MW00780726

THE RHETORIC OF TERROR

The Rhetoric of Terror

REFLECTIONS ON 9/11 AND
THE WAR ON TERROR

Marc Redfield

Fordham University Press

NEW YORK ‡ 2009

Copyright © 2009 Fordham University Press

All rights reserved. No part of this publication may be reproduced, stored in a retrieval system, or transmitted in any form or by any means—electronic, mechanical, photocopy, recording, or any other—except for brief quotations in printed reviews, without the prior permission of the publisher.

Fordham University Press has no responsibility for the persistence or accuracy of URLs for external or third-party Internet websites referred to in this publication and does not guarantee that any content on such websites is, or will remain, accurate or appropriate.

Library of Congress Cataloging-in-Publication Data

Redfield, Marc, 1958–
The rhetoric of terror : reflections on 9/11 and the war on terror / Marc Redfield.
     p.   cm.
Includes bibliographical references and index.
ISBN 978–0-8232–3123–2 (alk. paper)—ISBN 978–0-8232–3124–9 (pbk. : alk. paper)
     1. September 11 Terrorist Attacks, 2001.   2. Terrorism—Psychological aspects.   I. Title.
HV6432.7.R435   2009
363.325—dc22   2009020852

Printed in the United States of America
11 10 09   5 4 3 2 1
First edition

CONTENTS

ACKNOWLEDGMENTS

DRAFTS OF portions of the second chapter were given as short presentations at annual conferences hosted by the Modern Language Association and the North American Society for the Study of Romanticism during 2003 and 2004. Early and abbreviated versions of Chapters 1 and 2 were given as invited lectures during the years 2004 through 2006 at Brown University, Central Connecticut State University, Cornell University, the University of Ghent, McMaster University, the University of Pennsylvania, the University of Wisconsin at Madison, and Yale University. Related material was presented to a Sabbatical Fellows colloquium hosted by the American Philosophical Society. I am grateful to these many and various, but invariably attentive and helpfully critical audiences for helping me work out, clarify, and elaborate my arguments. My thanks also go to those students at Claremont Graduate University who discussed some of this material with me in a graduate seminar on terrorism, sovereignty, and literature in the spring of 2004.

Work on this project was supported by a CGU Faculty Research Award in 2004 and a sabbatical fellowship from the American Philosophical Society in 2006. At the time when the APS made its award, I was still conceiving of this book as a somewhat longer study more engaged with romantic-era and literary themes, and I can only hope that the then-co-executive officers of this wonderful institution, Richard S. and Mary Maples Dunn, will not be too disappointed by my having decided to focus attention largely on twenty-first-century issues.

Early and shorter versions or portions of these chapters have appeared as "War on Terror," in *Provocations to Reading: J. Hillis Miller and the Democracy to Come*, ed. Barbara Cohen and Dragan Kujund-žić (New York: Fordham University Press, 2005), 128–58, as "Virtual Trauma: The Idiom of 9/11," in *Diacritics*, and as "What's in a Name-Date? Reflections on 9/11," in *The Review of Education, Pedagogy, and Cultural Studies*. I thank the respective editors and publishers for permission to reprint these texts here.

Helen Tartar's support for this project has been unwavering, and my thanks to her are from the heart. David L. Clark and Samuel Weber read and commented on versions or portions of these chapters. Robert Klitgaard helped me figure out the right title. Jonathan Culler gave the entire text a careful reading and inspired me to write better concluding pages for it. My thanks go out as well to friends, colleagues, students, and family members who helped me in less specific but equally vital ways. Molly and Caroline sustain me always.

Since this book is about violence, loss, and mourning—mourning those whom we do not, cannot, never could "know"—I haven't wanted to dedicate it to any particular person. But after Jacques Derrida died, I was unable to compose sentences for this text without wanting to address and send them to him. Perhaps I wanted this all the more because my personal acquaintance with him had been modest. "Le géant qu'est Derrida," as Louis Althusser, who knew him a lot better, wrote in his memoirs while recalling the great philosophers of his era in France. Derrida was an unforgettable person, friend, and teacher, as so many have so often testified. I wish here simply to honor him with the name of philosopher: lover of wisdom, gadfly to the polis. More tirelessly than anyone I've ever known, he refused the lure of doxa and kept faith with thinking. *Amicus Plato sed magis amica veritas.*

THE RHETORIC OF TERROR

Introduction: Spectral Life and the Rhetoric of Terror

SURELY THERE COULD NOT BE, in our time, a book about 9/11 that did not originate in shock. Even the confession of a conspirator, one hypothesizes, would record somehow in its texture the impact of an event outstripping the imaginings of its perpetrators—even though one easily imagines the perpetrators imagining the attacks as precisely the kind of cinematic spectacle they went on to achieve. The shock of the attacks, inseparable from spectacle but irreducible to it, was registered (and thus partly absorbed) by the emergence of a name for this event: a bare name-date, "September 11," "9/11." Very quickly the name-date became a slogan, a blank little scar around which nationalist energies could be marshaled.

The two essays that comprise this book try to analyze how "9/11" unfolded and continues to unfold as a haunting event and why the language of war—of a putatively new kind of absolute war, a "war on terror"—so definitively closed down other possibilities for official response to this atrocity. Of course there are immediate and persuasive answers to those questions. The attacks haunt us because they were horrific; because they involved planes and skyscrapers, which form an essential part of modern life and in which we can feel particularly trapped and vulnerable; because they took place in the capital cities of a nation unused to suffering invasive violence; because they targeted and in one case utterly destroyed two prominent military and commercial symbols of the world's superpower. As for the idiom of war, since this superpower is famously jealous of its sovereignty, highly if erratically militarized in its culture, and, at the time of the attacks, governed by bellicose leaders, one would hardly expect it to have denied itself military acts of vengeance.

All this is obviously true. Any analysis, including mine, starts with such facts. But there is a strange density to the September 11 tragedy and the discourse of "war on terror" that emerged in its wake. So many overdetermined and overheated areas of modern Western culture jostle like tectonic plates at this intersection: the power of simulacra, media imagery, aesthetic spectacle; the "return of religion," piggybacking on an increasingly global if persistently uneven distribution of technological sophistication; the diffusion of quasi-sovereign power, the proliferation of ambiguous war zones, and the emergence of the charged, abjected figure of the "terrorist" in the U.S.-dominated late-twentieth-century world order. In setting out to examine the *rhetoric* of terror, I am not intending to study examples of politically persuasive speech, nor even (despite my interest in them) the slogan "war on terror" or the name-date "9/11" per se, but rather the cultural knot or wound that the name-date tries to name and that the deeply crazed notion of war on terror at least pretends to address.

The first part of this book risks the term "virtual trauma" to describe the ambiguous injury inflicted by the September 11 attacks *as mediated events*. "Virtual" is a word that has suffered a long, slow descent over the centuries, from its origins in the Latin *virtus* ("manliness, strength, virtue"). Some few hundred years ago, its various meanings narrowed down to "in effect," as opposed to full actuality, and in our day it has suffered further weakening via the phrase "virtual reality," such that it now connotes a certain fundamental fictionality and technicity.[1] As I use it here, "virtual" intends to suggest the trembling of an event on the edge of becoming present: one that is not fully or not properly "actual." A virtual threat would in this sense be one that has arrived without quite (yet) arriving—a death that, coming *then*, for others, and not yet *now*, for us, lays claim to us without literally or actually targeting us. Such virtuality therefore functions as both a consolation and a threat, retaining the power to haunt, sharing something of the force of the kind of wounding we call "traumatic." Yet, of course, we who watched TV were not, as a rule, traumatized in the technical, psychological sense or even in the more broadly idiomatic sense of having suffered abiding psychic damage—and if we then affirm that no real trauma can be said to have been produced in such a context, well, that, of course, is the principal connotation we now grant the adjective "virtual": something mediated, technically produced, not properly real. For those who had the protection of distance, the September 11 attacks were not "really" traumatic; they were a spectacle: a famously, infuriatingly cinematic spectacle.

Part of my argument in the first section of this book is that the attacks constituted virtual trauma not just because they relayed the threat, however improbable, of possible catastrophes to come (that was one of Jacques Derrida's main points when he was asked about the traumatic force of the attacks) but also because they constituted an event that *had* to be mediated.[2] I take this to be the meaning to be extracted from the much-remarked resemblance between the September 11 attacks and disaster movies: it is not so much that "they did it but we wished for it," to cite Jean Baudrillard's provocative if rather imperialistic formulation, as that the attacks took shape and took place in an environment (a place, a time, a culture, a global context) in which a spectacular act of terrorism could only occur as (the shock of) a scripted, predicted, mediated, disseminated spectacle.[3] The double strike on the World Trade Center, rather than that on the Pentagon, has always been felt to be the essence of "9/11." In my view, this is not just because the towers burned and collapsed so dramatically and damagingly (though that is a large part of it, of course: most of the victims of the day's attacks died in those towers) but because the socio-geographical space inhabited by the World Trade Center was (and is) so heavily mediatized, so utterly penetrated by representational technologies of global reach, and so symbolically at the heart of the world's various political, financial, and semiotic webs of power that the destruction of the towers could not help being at once the ultimate media event and (therefore) a haunting image of the deracinating force of communicational technology at work, disseminating images of disaster from the symbolic center of technological, capitalist, and national power. On a global or even a national scale, the material damage caused by the attacks was minute; once again, if we are to speak of cultural (as opposed to personal, psychological) trauma at all here, we have to say it was *virtual*. But "virtual" is not at all a synonym for insignificant or nonexistent. The sublime, all-too-aesthetic spectacle itself conveyed a hint of its own resistance to visual consumption, precisely because it so obscenely epitomized the workings of television: a technology that enacts for its viewers a dream of invulnerability—of Godlike seeing—yet in doing so displaces and de-realizes the events it "covers." Thus, in its having to be mediated, the event called 9/11 at once warded off and enacted the central paradox of technological reproduction, whereby a singular event—most poignantly, the deaths suffered by irreplaceable people, at a specific time and place—enters representation as reproducible, fungible, displaced, split off from itself.

Nationalism, I have argued elsewhere, works to cushion what Walter Benjamin calls the experience of shock, by which he means not just the barrage of stimuli we encounter in urban and more generally in modern life but the pressure of the technical processes that capture and document us, to the point of shaping us socially and psychically.[4] The nation, in Benedict Anderson's famous phrase, is an "imagined community" sustained by communicational technologies, yet since these deracinating technologies necessarily exceed the spatial and spiritual enclosure of the nation they enable, nationalism falls naturally into mournful, defensively aggressive postures.[5] The atavistic nationalism so prominent in U.S. political and mass-mediated culture has, in my view, much to do with the political, technical, and socioeconomic developments that led twentieth-century "mass culture" per se to be tagged as "American." And since the September 11 attacks not only violated the sovereign immunity of the world's superpower but in doing so effected something like a spectral wound in the fabric of mediation itself, they inevitably unleashed powerfully nationalist feelings and acts of mourning and anger. The attacks perhaps did not absolutely have to be treated by Congress and the Bush administration as acts of war calling for extralegal, military action (we are familiar with the pragmatic argument that careful police work and extant legal systems form by far the most effective defense against terrorism), but the U.S. "declaration of war on terror" was a thoroughly and fiercely overdetermined speech act.

My second chapter parses this phantasmatic performative by way of a meditation on sovereignty, drawing particularly (though not always uncritically) on Giorgio Agamben's interesting speculations on the proliferation of para-legal spaces, or states of exception, in the modern world. I read the declaration of war on terror as *the* exemplary speech act of sovereign power in a context in which sovereignty endures as a kind of afterimage of itself, dispersed into mobile, legally ambiguous sites of incarceration, police action, and war, while the U.S. bid for global hegemony finds its demonized other in deterritorialized, Al-Qaeda–style terrorism. The "terrorist" thereby becomes the abject double of the "sovereign"—he is above the law in his putative power to declare war ("they declared war on us, and we declared war back," as the Bush administration mantra had it), yet also therefore below all law, an instance of bare life to be either killed outright or made to disappear into a camp, where he will be interrogated and stored away—and perhaps occasionally put on display, hooded and shackled, his fluorescent prisonwear signaling the submission of the terrorist body not so much to the eye of the sovereign as to the gaze of a complexly differentiated global media apparatus that even a superpower can only court and manipulate, never really control.

Analyses of the sort I offer in these pages inevitably expose themselves to various kinds of misreading, so at the risk of being redundant let me be as clear as possible with regard to at least one essential point, in order to cramp as much as possible the arm-millings of the most reductive sort of response to theoretical critique. When, in the first half of this book, I try to work my way toward a notion of virtual trauma, I am referring such virtuality back to a terribly real crime, committed by members of a murderous organization, Al-Qaeda. And when, in the second half of this book, I write of the peculiar ghostliness of the "war on terror," I am addressing a spectrality inextricable from all sorts of real damage and horror. In the name of the war on terror—a war official enough to have a Washington acronym: GWOT (Global War on Terror)—the United States has invaded two countries; suffered, at present writing, over four thousand casualties while killing uncounted (and indeed, uncountable, given the politico-economic realities controlling the distribution of media and military resources) soldiers, guerrillas, and civilians; spent, at present writing, over half a trillion dollars conducting these military operations; rejected the Geneva Conventions; imprisoned suspects at will and for indefinite periods; tortured detainees and "rendered" others to be tortured by client states; spied on its own citizens, and on and on—nothing could be more real than the war on terror has been for these human beings. Or at least nothing could be more real than these innumerable and sometimes massive acts of violence, whereas few claims have come to seem less obvious than the Bush administration's assertion that the mounting wreckage of its tenure amounted to a "war on terror." Indeed, perhaps the administration itself did not always utterly believe its own slogans: a degree of venal strategizing doubtless entered into its promotion of this "war" as a means toward expanding executive privilege and the waging of expensive conventional wars against ("failed" and "rogue") sovereign states. Yet as I suggested above and argue at length in this book, the declaration and notion of war on terror is no simple diversion or mistake or illusion: it has deep roots in our culture and has had powerful effects on the world. That the war on terror is spectral does not in the least mean that it is not going on.

It is only superficially scandalous to claim that, since the Enlightenment, we have lived increasingly in a world of ghosts. Although only the world's privileged classes enjoy the sort of cocooning in simulacra that supposedly constitutes the "postmodern condition," very little in the world has remained untouched by capitalism and its technologies of production and distribution, communication and war, or by mutations of the ideas of nationalism, internationalism, and revolution that make up the intellectual and social landscape of modernity. In the developed world, near-magical technologies of inscription and transmission have made a certain mode of spectrality part of everyday experience: the voices, sounds, and images of vanished people, times, and places circulate constantly; the personifying dynamic of commodity fetishism conditions the texture of psychic, cultural, and socioeconomic life. Fictive persons called corporations saturate social and legal space, their actions usually having in the aggregate more consequence for both First and Third World populations than those of nation-states. Modernity's dominant theories of itself tend to be theories of phantom agency: the "invisible hand" at the heart of capitalism; the "reality of the appearance" stressed by the Marxist critique of ideology and commodity fetishism.

The U.S. war on terror, inconceivable apart from these broad technical, socioeconomic and cultural contexts, draws more specifically on a political history of the phantom. With the French Revolution, industrial development, and the rise of the working class, the specter of international, ideologically driven revolution emerged in tandem with the nation-state and the era of mass politics. To be sure, even conceived in narrowly political terms, the war on terror claims a long and wide-branching genealogical table, but I shall be arguing in this book that at least one important filament takes us back to Edmund Burke's counter-revolutionary writing from the 1790s, where we can observe, if not the hard-and-fast beginning of a Western war on terror (no hard-and-fast beginning could be adequate to such a war), at least one important place where the terms of a modern politics of paranoia are being sorted out and deployed. Marx and Engels summed up and sardonically appropriated this idiom in the famous opening sentence of *The Communist Manifesto* (1848): "A specter is haunting Europe—the specter of Communism."[6] For the next century and a half, that ghost loomed large in the spectral lives of capitalist societies, spurring various forms and acts of violence against an enemy who was understood to be fearsome precisely *as* a specter. In his account of repression and resistance during the military dictatorships in South America during the 1970s, Lawrence Weschler quotes a striking formulation of this topos of anticommunist rhetoric by the chief of staff of the Brazilian army at the Tenth Conference of American Armies in 1973:

> The enemy is undefined . . . it adapts to any environment, and uses every means, both licit and illicit, to achieve its aims. It disguises itself as a priest, a student or a campesino, as a defender of democracy or an advanced intellectual, as a pious soul or as an extremist protestor: it goes into the fields and the schools, the factories and the churches, the universities and the magistracy; if necessary, it will wear a uniform or civil garb; in sum, it will take on any role that it considers appropriate to deceive, to lie, and to take in the good faith of the Western peoples.[7]

Whether the Brazilian general believed his own hyperboles or was simply doing his bit to disseminate politically expedient fear is not the central point here. It is of the essence of haunting to be at once dubious and effective; one is not *supposed* to believe in ghosts—and indeed, skepticism is proper to haunting as a phenomenon. The phantom, like the fetish, passes untouched through the sieve of enlightened critique (as Slavoj Žižek once pungently characterized being in ideology: we know better, but we are doing it anyway).[8] Arguably a certain terror defines the very space of the political in modernity: a terror that, while historically and culturally determined and subject to all sorts of hypocritical manipulation and exploitation, nonetheless cannot simply be banished by an act of consciousness any more than the ghostly operations of market forces or the commodity form can be.

Beginning well before the fall of the Iron Curtain in 1989, the specter of the communist began to mutate into that of the Islamic terrorist in the Western media for a large number of empirical and ideological reasons. Although the racial and religious typecasting of this new enemy has worked to produce a seemingly more localizable threat than that provided by the communist menace, racial and religious profiling does not really uncover real terrorists, so the threat remains as mobile and resilient as ever, and in some ways more globalized than ever. Al-Qaeda may not be as decentralized and deterritorialized as is often imagined, but such imaginings, I have been suggesting, are an essential part of the "war." "The subject that haunts is not identifiable," Derrida comments; "one cannot see, localize, fix any form, one cannot decide between hallucination and perception, there are only displacements; one feels oneself looked at by what one cannot see."[9] The peculiarly frenzied new American style of coercive interrogation (many of its "techniques," as we know, borrowed wholesale from the playbook of the erstwhile totalitarian-communist enemy, with a leavening of abusive practices inspired mainly, so far as one can tell, by crude theorizing about "Arab masculinity") conveys the panic of a superpower unable to know and dominate its foe.[10] The major impression left by the string of war-on-terror torture scandals—Guantánamo, Abu Ghraib, the well-publicized cases of middle-class First World citizens kidnapped, "rendered," and tortured—has been one of not just indiscriminate but incompetent cruelty. These detainees, so often casually or mistakenly seized, are so often, as David Simpson observes, simply serving a role: "they stand for and stand in for an innumerable series of undiscovered figures of terror whose name is legion."[11] At Abu Ghraib, those special prisoners who never entered the official books but were brought in for interrogation by the CIA or its mercenaries and then made to disappear afterward were called "ghosts"; the same word was applied to their interrogators. And though the ghosts fled at the first hint of daylight, they left traces behind—screams overheard, a corpse glimpsed, sometimes a photograph circulating—for haunting is not a controllable phenomenon.[12]

No one parsed the uncontrollability of haunting more scrupulously than Derrida. Quoting the sentence from *Specters of Marx* that I cited above, David Simpson affirms, near the end of his important book *9/11: The Culture of Commemoration*, that "the figure of haunting and the paradigm of hauntology" that Derrida developed in the wake of the breakup of the Soviet Union in 1989 "perfectly encompass the epistemology of life in the face (but there is no face) of terrorism."[13] The present study shares that belief; indeed, I would add that Derrida's oeuvre in general—vast, protean, yet remarkably consistent over the half-century of its elaboration—has crucial resources to offer those who are trying to think about 9/11 and the war on terror. Derrida's groundbreaking philosophical analysis of iterability—iterability as the exposure to repetition with a difference elsewhere that makes all technics, signification, and psychic life possible—helps us understand why questions of mediation and aesthetics so rapidly become so fraught in our culture; why efforts to repress our essential political, psychic, and ontological vulnerability generate recursive spasms of violence; why a true call to peace can only take the form of hospitality toward the other, the specter. This book intends to be long on analysis and short on prescription, but my goal throughout is tacitly to suggest that the kind of thinking the Anglo-American academy calls "theory"—so often rhetorically identified with "terror," as we shall see—forms part of the tradition of modern cosmopolitan thought that runs from Kant to Derrida. My closing pages pledge allegiance somewhat more overtly to an ethics of cosmopolitanism. Nationalism is not simply or always a malign ideology, but under present circumstances I believe it to be an affliction the world could well be spared.

"One insight that injury affords is that there are others out there on whom my life depends, people I do not know and may never know," Judith Butler writes. "This fundamental dependency on anonymous others is not a condition that I can will away."[14] Nationalism is our culture's most potent mechanism for disavowing that fundamental dependency by, after a fashion, acknowledging it. Nationalism limits to its citizenry the anonymous others on whom it acknowledges dependence and marks out this limitation as a wound to be cherished: it is the source of an enmity toward the other and mourning for the self that serves to efface internal difference and generate national identity. Predicated on mourning, nationalism is a device for foreclosing mourning by sublimating the uniqueness and irreparability of each death suffered into the generality of a sacrifice. The specter is that which in death refuses sublimation. The specter, as a revenant, is a figure for or reiteration of iterability, yet the whole point, often insufficiently stressed in accounts of Derridean deconstruction, is that the specter returns because it is *singular*: because its life, figure, and voice are utterly irreplaceable. To affirm eirenic cosmopolitanism is to affirm that we are more vulnerable than we know and that we are haunted by voices, faces, and vulnerabilities that elude not only all documentation or border controls but indeed all recompense or acknowledgment. That is why they lay claim to us.

PART I

Virtual Trauma

. . . unterm

Datum des Nimmermenschtags im September

. . . under the

date of Nevermansday in September

—PAUL CELAN, "Huhediblu"

ALTHOUGH NO EVENT releases its full historical dimensions to those who endure it, the fact that the terrorist attacks of September 11 left a mark on ordinary language offers a hint of their historical force. A society of spectacle is necessarily an intensely if narrowly verbal society, and it is not just as an array of images but above all as a name that "September 11" has become part of everyday American cultural life. The photographs and video recordings remain on call in the archive, forever ready to reappear in the media or to be accessed via the Internet, but far more available, endlessly and unavoidably available, whether for purposes of quotidian communication or political manipulation, are the keywords themselves: the name-date, "September 11" or "9/11," and, shadowing it, an atomic-era military idiom, "ground zero," turned toponym. Speakers of American English can no more evade these newly minted proper names than they can the metaphysically and historically overburdened phrase "war on terror," which, in the name of "September 11," has provided the official gloss for so many acts of U.S. state violence since the fall of 2001.[1] More localized linguistic fallout from the attacks also exists, and may or may not turn out to hold interest for cultural analysts or historians.[2] But no cultural study of the September 11 attacks and their aftermath, whatever the methodology or emphasis, can afford to ignore the rhetorical and political work performed by this event's loomingly proper names—particularly the

13

name-date itself, for which no synonyms exist and which anchors all talk and all analysis of "September 11" to a powerful, haunting catachresis.

These names reiterate the trauma to which they point, and a close reading of them will help us approach the difficult question of how and why September 11 registers as a cultural trauma. That the attacks inflicted a shock of historical scale seems clear, but the shape and scope of this wound is not. The pain and damage suffered by survivors, victims, and the relatives and friends of victims of this atrocity is, of course, unquestionable: such suffering demands infinite respect and not, except in the privacy of the clinic, analysis. But if we try to conceive of trauma on a cultural level, things become more ambiguous, above all in the case of the 9/11 attacks. They were not of a society-threatening scale (as warfare, genocide, famine, or natural cataclysm have been for so many human societies), and the literal damage they did to the military and commercial orders symbolized by the Pentagon and the World Trade Center was minuscule. It is, of course, as symbolic acts of violence that they claim culturally traumatic status. But even here the symptoms are complex. In targeting and in one case destroying two prominent architectural symbols of a superpower, the terrorists do indeed seem to have managed to do some local damage to the process of symbolization itself. Their violence would thus have produced a "silence that is not mere mutism but intricately related to representation," to recall one of Dominick LaCapra's reflections on historical trauma (in this case, the Shoah).[3] Trauma involves blockage: an inability to mourn, to move from repetition to working through. It is certainly plausible that hyperbolic commemorative efforts such as those on display in "9/11 discourse" (as I shall call it) are in fact testimonials to blockage; for that matter it is plausible that a public sphere as saturated by consumerist and military interests as that of the present-day United States has no viable mechanisms for effective public grieving. Yet to say this is also to say that in such a context the very notion of cultural trauma becomes somewhat spectral and uncertain. Wherever one looks in 9/11 discourse, trauma and the warding off of trauma blur into each other, as the event disappears into its own mediation. All traumatic events arguably do this, but, as many have commented, there is something particularly virtual and hyperreal about the central "9/11" event—the World Trade Center catastrophe. To those not immediately threatened by it, this disastrous spectacle could seem at the time at once horrifically present and strangely unreal—"like a movie," as the saying went, another phrase I want to examine in detail—and years later this feeling of spectral pressure has only grown stronger. We have witnessed, on the one hand, a constant remembering and rememorializing of September 11 in publications and media events, political sloganeering, security controls, etc.; on the other hand—but is it an other hand?—such an avalanche of sickening images and narratives parading by under the banner of America's "war on terror"—Afghanistan, Guantánamo, Baghram, Abu Ghraib, the ongoing slaughter in Iraq—that the spectacular horror of 9/11 can sometimes seem strangely wan and distant on the horizon, nearly buried under the mounting wreckage. The event called September 11 or 9/11 was as real as death, but its traumatic force seems nonetheless inseparable from a certain ghostliness, not just because the attacks did more than merely literal damage (that would be true of any event causing cultural trauma) but because the symbolic damage done itself seems spectral—not unreal by any means, but not simply "real" either.

In what follows I shall be working my way toward a notion of *virtual* trauma by exploring a few of the ways in which images, videos, and televised transmissions made the destruction of planes and buildings and the killing of nearly three thousand people into "September 11." The name-date itself, I suggest, stages a double movement of inscription and effacement such that an act of naming becomes isomorphic with the structure of traumatic damage, on the one hand, and with the workings of technical reproducibility and mass mediation, on the other. I shall be drawing at a few crucial points on writings by two authors, Jacques Derrida and Susan Sontag, who both in their very different ways invested a lifetime in thinking about mediation, wounding, and mourning. Derrida's work in particular—which attends so relentlessly to paradoxes of singularity, iterability, and the event; to the pressure of virtuality upon presence; and to the deep structures of teletechnological being-in-the-world—can help us understand both the rhetorical power of the name "September 11," and the ways in which this name registers a trauma *of* mediation and transmission.[4] As a hypermediated event, September 11 makes legible modern society's formidably ambivalent relationship to the representational technologies that saturate it, and thus the question of what's in a name leads rapidly—indeed, in principle, immediately—to questions about the aesthetics and politics of mediation.

I. SEPTEMBER 11

What does it signify that a date has become a name? Name-dating in general tends to be a modern phenomenon, associable with what Benedict Anderson calls the "homogeneous empty time" of the nation-state and with the performative declaration of independence that brings a modern (and especially a postcolonial) state into being.[5] Despite their proximity to such sovereign performatives, however, name-dates tend to be unofficial names (legally, "the Fourth of July" is "Independence Day," and "le 14 juillet" is "la Fête Nationale"). Certainly in the case of "September 11" no official speech act was involved: the name-date rose like foam from the churning of the mass media in the days immediately following the attacks and has since become, to my knowledge, the only available term for these attacks worldwide, though American usage has its peculiarities. Elsewhere in the world the name-date often acquires an explanatory tag that makes for a less melodramatic synecdoche: "the attacks of 11 September 2001"; *die Anschläge vom 11. September*; etc. But where American or American-inflected English is being spoken, the name-date "September 11" usually surfaces in its purity—no descriptive supplement, no year—and then reduces further to numerical representation: 9/11. Rendered numerically, the term becomes an even more sharply American idiom, for it depends on and makes rhetorical capital out of the U.S. convention of citing the month before the day in numerical dating: "11/9" would not pack the rhythmic punch that the double-trochee hammer-blows of "9/11" do. (William Blake's poem "The Tyger" offers English literature's most famous example of this kind of hypnotic trochaic rhythm.) In most of the United States and Canada, the numbers 9–1-1 have the further subliminal force of composing the telephone number for emergency help: this triple digit, since its adoption in 1968, has been drilled into the consciousnesses of most inhabitants of the American landmass north of Mexico.[6] Indeed, presumably because of the homology between this number and the American way of writing a date, in 1987 President Reagan proclaimed September 11 to be "9-1-1 Emergency Telephone Number Day." (How much of this was known by the planners of the 9/11 attacks is uncertain: obsessed though they were with the symbolism of their violence, they do not seem to have granted particular importance to the date of their operation.[7]) From 1987 to 2001, "9-1-1 Day" was celebrated in modest ways in many communities in the United States as a way to promote safety awareness; after the attacks, "9-1-1 Day" was dropped from the official calendar. On October 25, 2001, the U.S. Congress dubbed September 11 a "National Day of Prayer and Remembrance," and on September 4, 2002, President Bush changed this sober if unmemorable appellation to "Patriot Day" (a name that implicitly forbids mourning, while covering with yet one more shovelful of cultural forgetfulness the 316 victims of the attacks who were not U.S. citizens).

None of these official christenings, however, has made much of a dent in public consciousness, and the odds are good that they never will. The name-date "September 11" has too much rhetorical power. This power stems from its blankness, its empty formality as inscription: an emptiness that works in at least two contradictory ways. On the one hand, like "the Fourth of July" or any other sort of name-date, "September 11" presupposes and demands knowledge: "September 11"—the year understood, the attacks understood. Imperatively and imperialistically, the empty date suggests itself as a zero point, the ground of a quasi-theological turn or conversion: *everything changed* that day, as the U.S. mainstream media so often tells itself. A new history begins here, at this calendrical ground zero: previous September 11s disappear into that zero, from the bureaucratically trivial ("9-1-1 Day") to the historical and tragic (September 11, 1973, the date of Salvador Allende's overthrow in a U.S.-backed coup that ushered in one of the worst reigns of terror in the twentieth century). The phrase "September 11" presents itself as a constative, if deictic, description (it was *that* very day) that simultaneously unfolds as a performative, an imperial command (you shall have no other September 11s; should you mention others, they will be secondary to this absolute, toxic *punctum*: if you wish, say, to refer to Chile, you will have to speak of "the *other* September 11").[8] This performative force, in other words, cannot be distinguished from political, cultural, technological, military, and socioeconomic force. The formal minimalism of the name-date would be nugatory in its effects were it not for the name-date's endless repetition as a mantra within a consumer culture within which all other dates, times, places, acts, or meanings melt into air. Before or after September 11, 2001, very few U.S. citizens could have been counted on to know, for example (and it is an exemplary example), what September 11 means in Chilean history. The naked phrase "September 11" rhetorically reperforms that ignorance, and the global hegemony of American media and culture imposes the sign of that erasure worldwide. And each time we now say "September 11," we repeat, however momentarily or provisionally, this act of effacement and presupposition. The name-date cannot be mentioned without being used, even if one's intent, as here, is analytical and critical.

Yet that performative persistence or excess also gives criticism its chance. If, on the one hand, the formal emptiness of the phrase "September 11" imposes knowledge and amnesia, knowledge *as* amnesia—a memory projected against the ground zero of a hyperbolic forgetting—on the other hand, this same formal emptiness registers and even loudly proclaims a trauma, a wound beyond words: an inability to say what this violence, this spectacle, this "everything changing," *means*. A name-date like "the Fourth of July" commemorates a felicitous (if complex) speech act possessing relatively obvious consequences; but the name-date "September 11" gestures toward obscurity. If American usage, in its minimalism, hints that "September 11" or "9/11" signifies more than "the attacks" per se, what is this *more*? The sheer iteration of a date thus performs not just an imperious and quasi-theological act of erasure and inscription but also, at the same time, a stutter, a gasp of incomprehension. Derrida, in his interview with Giovanna Borradori on October 22, 2001, suggested that the imperative to speak of "9/11" was inseparable from a nagging incomprehension:

Who or what gives us this threatening order (others would already say this terrorizing if not terrorist imperative): name, repeat, re-name "September 11," "le 11 septembre," even when you do not yet know what you are saying and are not yet thinking what you refer to in this way. . . . what remains "infinite" in this wound, is that we do not know what it is and so do not know how to de-scribe, identify, or even name it.[9]

Derrida went on to make that assertion more concrete. The "event" signaled by the name-date resists comprehension and the work of mourning both insofar as it is felt as a threat to the global and mani-fold work of accreditation performed by American power and as a threat that has not yet arrived. The first point stresses the mutual inseparability of economic, military, technical, and discursive orders within the "world order" that "since the 'end of the Cold War' . . . in its relative and precarious stability, depends largely on the solidity and reliability, on the *credit* of American power. . . . Hence, to desta-bilize this superpower, which plays at least the "role" of the guardian of the prevailing world order, is to risk destabilizing the entire world, including the declared enemies of the United States" (93). This destabilization extends to "the system of interpretation, the axi-omatic, logic, rhetoric, concepts, and evaluations that are supposed to allow one to comprehend and to explain something like 'Septem-ber 11'" (ibid.). Derrida's second point is that this rent in the global web of accreditation is also a temporal wound, for to the extent that the event is traumatic, it has in a sense not yet fully arrived and is never present to itself: "There is traumatism with no possible work of mourning when the evil comes from the possibility to come of the worst, from the repetition to come—though worse" (97). If one knew, Derrida proposes, that "September 11" would never happen again, then the horror of the attacks could be named, understood, historicized, and put to rest; insofar as the attacks produce trauma, they do so as figures of a threat to come, from the future.

This futural inflection of trauma may also be read in the name-date—the month-day minus the year. When we add the year, we fix the date in calendrical history; when we omit it we obtain the vibrant urgency of a date that recurs, that insists on its recurrence. Let us stay with Derrida's thought a little longer, for the paradox of the date recurs frequently in his work as a version of his great theme of singularity and iterability, particularly in *Shibboleth* (1986), his short book on Paul Celan. The date names the one time, the finite event that happens once, only once—and yet to name this once, to be read-able *as* a date, the date must efface its singularity, split itself and repeat itself elsewhere. "How can one date what does not repeat if dating also calls for some form of return, if it recalls in the readability of a repetition? But how can one date anything other than that which never repeats itself?"[10] To be itself, the date must efface the singular-ity of which it speaks. A date thus finds itself "carried away, trans-ported," in becoming itself:

> A date marks itself and becomes readable only in freeing itself from the singularity that it nonetheless recalls. It is readable in its ideality; its body becomes an ideal object: always the same, through the different experiences that point to or constitute it, objective, guaranteed by codes. This ideality carries forgetting into memory, but it is the memory of forgetting itself, the truth of forgetting. (35)

Which is also to say that the date is of and for the future: "The date is a future anterior: it gives the time one assigns to anniversaries to come" (25). A date is always already moving beyond itself, a move-ment that is also the mark of its finitude: its essential forgettability. It is of the essence of a date that its significance can be perverted or forgotten. To name an event "September 11" is to make the event into its own memorial, always-already memorized, at least in part (U.S. schoolchildren of the future, learning the event as its date, will only need to add the year), but also its own annulment. If all proper names, as Derrida has often noted, bear death within them—their essence being to survive their referent, to be iterable elsewhere, past the life to which they refer—the name-date exacerbates this predica-ment, reconsigning itself to self-forgetfulness with every commemo-rative iteration.

The name-date "September 11" draws its power from this vi-brantly contradictory motion away from and toward its referent. At one and the same time it commemorates and preserves a past event for a future recollection, recalls the futurity that renders this past traumatic, hints at its own forgetfulness and forgettability, and effaces the effacement of the singularity and finitude that opens the space of its possibility. Moving away from itself, the name-date erects itself into a fetish precisely because it is always naming its own loss. It thus becomes a compulsively repeated slogan. This compulsion to repeat, to mention and use over and over again the name-date "September 11," is a specific instance of the more general commemorative frenzy that characterizes 9/11 discourse. A passion to document this event, in numerous media—I shall come back in a moment to questions of media and mediation—has driven most displays of public mourning, from early efforts such as the "Portraits of Grief" project of the *New York Times* and the ambitiously inclusive *Here Is New York* photography exhibit, to the variously commemorative activities addressing or coinciding with September 11's fifth anniversary: dozens more books of widely varying quality, perspective, and commercial ambition; two photograph collections titled *Aftermath*;[11] two big-budget films; a TV miniseries and any number of documentaries and talking-head programs; special issues of magazines; installations and commemorations (most notably the opening of the World Trade Center Memorial Museum, which on August 22, 2006, began posting large photographs on the "Ground Zero fence"); the recent release of the North American Aerospace Defense Command (NORAD) and other transcripts and audio files; a spike in the media coverage of the ongoing political and commercial struggle over Ground Zero as real estate and as commemoration site; and so on. The corporate media form only part of the September 11 memory industry: scholarly and alternative media have remained steadily active in this field, and the literature on 9/11 as a U.S. government–backed conspiracy has become gigantic.[12] Even Al-Qaeda, in quest of media attention as the fifth anniversary neared, released a "commemorative" video of bin Laden and some of the planners of the September 11 attacks—including two of the hijackers—engaging in paramilitary and martial-arts drills.[13]

No one is in any danger of forgetting September 11—and yet it is precisely this danger, which is also an ambivalent desire (a desire to forget, a desire to forget that one has desired to forget, a desire to forget certain things and not others), that drives this vast representational and commemorative machine. In this respect, of course, September 11 is no different from any other cultural or personal catastrophe: all mourning grapples with economies of memory and forgetting; all events undergo winnowing in becoming historical. Cultural memory, as we know, is ongoing cultural-political contestation. Like all historical—which is to say, finite, forgettable—events, the attacks of September 11 provoke interminable interpretation. If there is a difference here, it has to do with the ferocity with which this event announces its inseparability from its mediation or transmission—beginning, as we have seen, with its name. The name-date makes meaning around a wound that, in the context of naming, is the wound of sheer, blank randomness: this event just happened to happen on *that* day. Both personal and national identity, it has been argued, are haunted by unacknowledgable melancholia—by a disavowal of the self's and the community's dependence on and responsibility for others. And if, like Judith Butler, we affirm that "part of what I am is the enigmatic traces of others," and therefore that I am constituted partly "by those whose deaths I disavow, whose nameless and faceless deaths form the melancholic background for my social world, if not my First Worldism," it becomes tempting to read "September 11"'s imperialistic repression of Chile's September 11—for which the United States was so proximately responsible—as a prime instance of nation-sustaining melancholia.[14] Perhaps it is this, but if so, this constitutive melancholia itself depends on the sheer randomness of an event and a dating system. The nameless and faceless deaths of the other, infinitely numerous, endlessly ungrievable, are at once opened and foreclosed for us, here, by way of a material sign. The tragedy called "September 11" names itself as a drive to repeat, remember, and forget—names itself as an impossible work of mourning, confessing itself as such, yet at the same forgetting itself and becoming, with terrible ease and effectiveness, an occasion for the violent denegation of loss and the rallying cry for a phantasmatic, absolute war.

2. GROUND ZERO

Like "September 11," the term "Ground Zero" emerged quasi-spon-
taneously as a proper name in the American mass media immediately
after the attacks. As a proper name, uncontextualized and capitalized, it refers to the site formerly occupied by the World Trade Center towers; as an idiom in more general use, it refers to the impact
point of a bomb or the exact locus of an explosion. The term was
military jargon when it was used at the Trinity site during the development and testing of the atom bomb; after the bombing of Hiroshima and Nagasaki, it entered the American sociolect and is now
commonly used to describe centers of devastation, natural or man-
made.[15] Just as there is now only one "September 11," there is now
only one "Ground Zero," capitalized. But the latter term has been
torn not out of the calendar but out of the lexicon of atomic warfare—its erasure of the past bears a more visibly historical stamp.
Here the melancholic aura limning a nation-state seeking to "recon-
stitute its imagined wholeness,"[16] while denying its own vulnerability
and half-remembering its own murderous past, is more in evidence.
"Ground Zero" both calls up and wards off the ghost of Hiroshima,
remembering that other scene of destruction while also distancing or
demoting it by rendering it an *other* ground zero.[17] Yet in pointing
to the past—to another atrocity (this one with victims in the hun-
dreds of thousands) and another horrific spectacle (carefully photographed and measured, let us not forget, by one of the B-29s making
up the U.S. bombing unit, the 509th Composite Group, which deliv-
ered the Hiroshima and Nagasaki bombs)—this term also points to
the future: to the nuclear bomb that, since the 1950s, has hung in
American skies, waiting to fall. And just as "Ground Zero" appropriates and effaces the past, it appropriates and effaces the future.
Invoking the nuclear threat, it imagines the future *as* past, and as
imaginable. The hammer blow has fallen: Ground Zero itself has
appeared in the world—and yet we have survived. Thus "the worst,"
in Derrida's phrasing (or at least a version of the worst) is at once
conjured up and conjured away.

The term "Ground Zero" stems from and exemplifies a rhetoric
and praxis of *targeting* that Samuel Weber, building on Heidegger's

interpretation of modern technics, diagnoses as decisive for the Western metaphysical tradition generally and as particularly on display in the militarized national culture of the United States after World War Two.[18] From Plato onward, Weber suggests, thinking has been construed as "hitting the mark, making the point" (viii), and the late twentieth century has witnessed a palpable inflation of the concept and praxis of technical, representational, and military targeting. To mention only one example—an important and literally military example—consider the technology and fantasy of so-called precision bombing. Particularly prominent in the military-political idiom of the United States, Great Britain, and Israel, the notion of the surgical strike represents a kind of fetishized targeting of the gesture of targeting itself, whereby the precise identification and attainment of a target doubles as a moral justification of the destruction being unleashed. The "smart bomb," whether or not it hits its intended victim, almost always kills innocents. But its *intention* was precise, and the statesman or military spokesperson need only issue an assurance that the act of targeting had been as precise as possible. In such a context, the Bush administration's (and, it must be said, the mainstream U.S. media's) post–September 11 embrace of preemptive strikes and assassinations represents little more than a modest ratcheting up of established First World and particularly U.S. practice. And since the need to find targets and test new technologies in fact drives this "politics of good intentions," the good intentions can now and then become manifestly disposable supplements, as in Donald Rumsfeld's famous suggestion, offered immediately after September 11, that the U.S. bomb Iraq rather than Afghanistan—not, in this case, because Iraq was imagined to have had anything to do with the attacks, but simply because it had better targets.[19]

The name "Ground Zero" reverses the direction of the targeting process: *they* targeted *us*. They struck with precision, hitting the symbolic Center (of World Trade) and transforming it into a Zero. But since—particularly from the perspective of the nationalist discourse that was hyperenergized by the attacks—the "we" has survived, they also missed as they hit. The zero is a ground, American ground, the virgin space of a new beginning ("everything changed"), the guarantee of a wounded innocence and a good conscience.[20] Having been targeted, we may and must now target the enemy. The fantasies and anxieties of the "war on terror" have everything to do with targeting, of course—with locating, identifying, giving a face and a name to the enemy. Large metaphysical issues lurk here. To target is to frame and locate an object in relation to a sovereign subject: thus Weber's analysis relays Heidegger's identification of modern technics as the culmination of metaphysics. The subject, by constituting itself as masterful in targeting an other, wards off its finitude—its exposure to death, chance, failure, limitation, singular times and places. And yet, the more powerful the technologies of targeting, the more evanescent and mobile the target can become. The subject's empowerment is at once genuine and phantasmatic: technology puts the world on order for a will to power, yet the more the world becomes put on order, *gestellt*, the more objects disappear into an unmasterable network of relationships and the more the subject becomes subjected to the *Ge-stell*.[21] The "war on terror," with its paranoid invocation of a shadowy enemy threatening national security, may in this sense be interpreted along Heideggerian lines as a symptom of the culmination of metaphysics.[22] The "we" and the "they," however violently differentiated on racial and religious grounds, nonetheless blur ("they" are "here," using our technology, hiding in plain sight, like the communists and anarchists before them; "we" are "there," running our global business, and now had better send more of us "there," take the fight "there," etc.).

The name "Ground Zero" stokes a fantasy of omnipotence that is inseparable from vulnerability and exposure. When the nation becomes a ground zero—or, more precisely, in its survival, its newly frenetic living on, a *beyond* of ground zero—the nation becomes a "Homeland" needing ever more stringent securing.[23] And if the Homeland can never be protected enough, this is precisely because, in a teletechnologized world, it cannot secure its *location*. The *9/11 Commission Report* indirectly confesses as much, albeit in the traditional language of geopolitical strategizing: "9/11 has taught us that terrorism against American interests 'over there' should be regarded just as we regard terrorism against America 'over here.' In this same sense, the American homeland is the planet" (362). If a certain imperialism or state terrorism speaks here, so too does a terrorized, paranoid subject, conscious on some level that it has no home, only

constitutively inadequate, if politically useful, technologies and dis-
courses of security, deployed within an ambivalent state of
emergency.[24]

3. LIKE A MOVIE

A certain transcendence is thus built into "September 11" and
"Ground Zero" as speakable proper names.[25] To speak them and
claim them, one has to feel shadowed or marked by the event to
which they refer, yet of course one also has to have survived—to
have been, if only minimally, elsewhere at the time. All testimony
presupposes a minimal distance from the event: hence the claim,
familiar from Holocaust studies, that acts of witnessing must sustain
themselves in the shadow of a certain impossibility.[26] But in the
names given to the atrocity we are considering here, predicaments
general to catastrophic experience become self-consciously the material of a particular representation: "September 11," as we saw earlier,
conjures up an unsteady play of forgetting and remembering;
"Ground Zero"—a toponym manifestly evocative of obliteration and
living on—at once feeds the fantasy of the subject's omnipotence,
forecloses the work of mourning, and sustains an abiding anxiety.

It is possible to be more specific about the general manner of the
survival of this particular speaking subject. Most people who experienced September 11 did so not as survivors or eyewitnesses but as
TV watchers, who tuned in either during the real time of the attacks
or in the hours after they occurred. If the term "Ground Zero" inher-
ently privileges the events in New York over those in Pennsylvania
and at the Pentagon, this is congruent with our sense that September
11 *was* essentially, *as* "September 11," the spectacular attack on and
collapse of the towers of the World Trade Center. Surely there has
never been a more utterly mediated event. The hijackers attacked a
point in world space so saturated with camera coverage that video
footage and sequential still shots exist even of the *first* plane, American 11, smashing into the north face of the north tower at 8:46 A.M.[27]
Three minutes later, at 8:49 A.M., CNN had live feed established.
Though the Internet played a significant role in disseminating news
of the attacks—David Levi Strauss claims that on September 11
"more people clicked on documentary news photographs than on

pornography for the first (and only) time in the history of the Internet"—the main medium of transmission was television.[28] It is estimated that by the end of the day as many as two billion people worldwide had seen footage of the burning and collapsing towers. The military and the Federal Aviation Authority (FAA) learned of the attacks by watching television, like practically everyone else. ("It's on the world news," one stunned voice says on the recently released NORAD tapes. And at the peak of the confusion and tragedy, with ghost planes being chased and with "everyone staring at CNN on the overhead screen," a weapons technician can be heard to say, "OK—let's watch our guys. . . . Not the TV."[29]) Lethally real, of course, for those who were actually at Ground Zero, the event was nonetheless so peculiarly, radically mediatized that, according to these published accounts, for many hours federal and military agencies got their only reliable information via television.

And what was unfolding on television in turn seemed akin to a particular cinematic genre: the big-budget disaster movie. Wherever one looks in 9/11 discourse, from the high-theoretical (if well-circulated) analyses of Jean Baudrillard or Slavoj Žižek to the unrehearsed comments of eyewitnesses, one finds references to this resemblance between reality and semblance, more specifically, between reality and this particular kind of Hollywood product. In a recent *New York Review of Books* article, for instance, the classicist and culture critic Daniel Mendelson describes his own real-life experience of seeing the first plane hit the north tower: "at the time, the first, irrational thought that came into my staggered mind was that someone was making a blockbuster disaster movie. What I thought, in fact, was this: In this day and age, with its sophisticated digital special effects, why would anyone use *real* planes?"[30]

Žižek, in an early and incisive commentary (a version of which circulated on the Internet a few weeks after the attacks), makes a more intellectually developed version of this point from the perspective of the more distant spectator: "when we watched the oft-repeated shot of frightened people running toward the camera ahead of the giant cloud of dust from the collapsing tower, was not the framing of the shot itself reminiscent of spectacular shots in a catastrophe movie, a special effect which outdid all others, since . . . reality is the best appearance of itself?"[31] Not all aspects of the World Trade Center attacks were experienced as uncannily scripted by spectators, and clearly the experiences of most survivors and many close eyewitnesses were not even remotely cinematic. But the resemblance between this real-life disaster and the cinematic spectacles of the corporate dream-machine are neither accidental nor trivial.[32] Even in a mundanely literal sense, it is possible that cinema assisted the imagining of these attacks before they occurred: it comes as no surprise to hear that Osama bin Laden's associates watched Hollywood disaster movies in their Afghan compound while brainstorming attack strategies (or that, in the wake of 9/11, the Pentagon and the White House enlisted Hollywood directors and executives to help them imagine future terrorist strikes).[33]

Yet if, on the one hand, the simile "like a movie" emerges out of a specific historical, cultural, economic, and technological context—one in which a certain kind of high-tech, highly capitalized, globally distributed cinematic product becomes associated with the technical production of scenes of spectacular destruction—it is clear that this simile functions above all to communicate the speaker's sense of the seeming unreality of the event being described. "After four decades of big-budget Hollywood disaster films," Susan Sontag suggests, " 'it felt like a movie' seems to have displaced the way survivors of a catastrophe used to express the short-term unassimilability of what they had gone through: 'It felt like a dream.' "[34] Catastrophic experiences outstrip understanding: disrupting the habitual ways we make sense of the world, they feel unreal precisely because they are overwhelming. Not that those who saw a "movielike" spectacle were necessarily undergoing trauma in a medical sense—indeed, probably very few were. Those who suffered genuinely traumatic shock would surely in most cases be those who, either physically or psychologically too close to Ground Zero, did not have the luxury of seeing a spectacle that was "like a movie." The simile posits a viewer at a crucial (if in some cases physically minimal) distance from the buildings; furthermore, as a simile, it both registers something shocking and cushions the shock, assimilating the unassimilable to the known. We have seen it before; movies have prepared us for this: like anxiety-formations in Freud, they have drawn the sting of the future by anticipating the disaster to come. To feel the uncanny pressure of a script or genre on one's life is to register but also ward off the impact of an event.

I risk the term "virtual trauma" here to denote not a condition of psychological damage but rather a making legible, within the medium itself, of a violence inherent to all media technologies, which record and remember the unique only by effacing and forgetting it. There is a risk to this usage, for such trauma is not entirely "real" insofar as it works to ward off psychic trauma. Sufferers from posttraumatic stress disorder are not spectators: possessed by an event, they endure preternaturally literal repetitions of it as hallucinatory flashbacks, nightmares, and daydreams.[35] Audiovisual media technologies transform such literal repetition into a kind of subjective power. Thanks to a machine, a prosthesis, one has repeatability on hand. Time and space become objects to be targeted and archived. Far from suffering traumatic damage, the subject of technics seems if anything to have put trauma to work—and yet, as we noted earlier while considering the logic and rhetoric of targeting, technical empowerment is always also disenfranchisement, the prosthesis a wounding supplement. Representational power produces a residue of uncertainty precisely because it re-presents something singular, thereby enabling the archive as the possibility of history as fiction. As Sontag more concretely puts it: "something becomes real—to those who are elsewhere, following it as 'news'—by being photographed. But a catastrophe that is experienced will often seem eerily like its representation."[36] And in late-twentieth- and early-twenty-first-century American culture, that potential falseness, when operative in a certain context of spectacular violence, receives the signifier *movie*. A "war photograph seems inauthentic, even though there is nothing staged about it, when it looks like a still from a movie" (78). The World Trade Center attacks insist on this figure. Repetition elsewhere and elsewhen being precisely the phenomenon it describes, the simile "like a movie" can be reevaluated as often as one cares to replay footage of the sort Žižek has in mind out of the stocks of CNN video lodged throughout the Internet.

This strange overlap of the virtual and the real takes a number of forms throughout the event of September 11. On the NORAD tapes, for instance, voices ask repeatedly, "Is this real-world or exercise?"— for the attacks coincided with a military exercise that in fact was to feature a hijacking.[37] In a technologically saturated world, the difference between the test drive and the real thing, the simulacrum and the referent, blurs. The difference between them can be, as here, a matter of life and death; indeed, as here, the difficulty of *reading* that difference can be a matter of life and death. No competent theorist of textuality or postmodernity has ever imagined otherwise: the urgency of the need to distinguish between image and referent is directly proportionate to the uncertainty of their interpenetration. This uncertainty generates the sort of anxiety legible in the furious denunciations of postmodern relativism and irony that so many cultural critics felt driven to utter in the wake of the attacks,[38] also in the energetic construction of conspiracy theories that rediscover, with whatever degree of imaginative recklessness, a reality behind appearances—a reality that can be identified, named, and *targeted*. If in traumatic experience uncertainty manifests itself as a dimension of the wound suffered, "September 11" persistently presents itself, as we have seen, as a kind of trauma without trauma, as an event that can only be named by its date, located at an unrepresentable zero point, sacralized as a revelation and point of origin yet talked about as a (false, illusory) real-life movielike spectacle. The real-world damage done—vast enough, though of modest proportion when measured quantitatively against so many other atrocities—is persistently encoded as mediated, transmitted damage.

Damage mediated is always potentially damage falsified, and not just in an epistemological sense. Consumer society understands the media representations that it ravenously consumes as fundamentally violent, voyeuristic, pornographic. The camera that records suffering provides a supplemental violation, an obscene repetition of injury. The WTC attacks brought a commonplace of televisual society into the sharpest possible focus. On the one hand, the phrase "it was like a movie" conjures up not just an excess of event over believability but a sense that this event *is to be mediated*, would have no sense, perhaps would not even have occurred if it were not being recorded and transmitted. (For of course, this particular act of terrorism was utterly dedicated to the camera, down to the lag between the first and the second strike, making possible maximum media coverage. If all terrorism is symbolic violence that depends on some mechanism of transmission or dissemination, the WTC attacks raise a general characteristic of the genre to which they belong to a new power.[39]) On the other hand, the cameras and transmitters repeat the terroristic violation of human dignity itself, reducing someone's pain and death to an image, stripping away the soul in capturing a representation of the body.

The press manages this ambivalence by splitting itself into reporting and entertainment, but for fundamental reasons, documentary photographers—however personally courageous, however necessary their work—can never operate at a guaranteed distance from the paparazzi against whom they (quite legitimately) define themselves. This ambivalence was literally part of the spectacle of September 11. An extraordinary number of amateurs and professionals at or near the scene recorded the tragedy with still and video cameras, as the *Here Is New York* photography exhibit and Web site testifies (there is an entire subgenre of 9/11 pictures of people taking pictures), while both the government and the corporate media waffled on what to show and what to censor, and officials and rescue workers on-site reacted at times with anger at the spectacle of a spectacle being filmed. As Tom Junod, in "Falling Man," his famous article about the representation of "jumpers" comments:

> The resistance to the image—to the images—started early, started immediately, started on the ground. A mother whispering to her distraught child a consoling lie: "Maybe they're just birds, honey." Bill Freehan, second in command at the fire department, chasing a bystander who was panning the jumpers with his video camera, demanding that he turn it off, bellowing, "Don't you have any human decency?"

Junod argues that "in the most photographed and videotaped day in the history of the world, the images of people jumping were the only images that became, by consensus, taboo" in the U.S. media (elsewhere in the world they did not). That is an overstatement. The "jumpers" do indeed seem to have touched a nerve in American society and inspired the strictest gestures of self-censorship in the corporate media, but even they had their images recorded on television (momentarily, before the networks realized what they were filming) and published in newspapers (for a day, September 12, before being pulled). more to the point, even they (indeed, *especially* they) could always become a locus of fascination and of moralizing language about the importance of bearing witness, as Junod's well-received article demonstrates.[40] Where there is censorship there is desire. The jumpers were at the epicenter of a wider economy of ambivalence, within which frenzied representational activity coexisted with official and unofficial acts of negation. Mayor Giuliani's formal attempt to ban photography near Ground Zero was brief, but informal, quasi-spontaneous, and uneven gestures of censorship persisted and left their mark on every aspect of the September 11 phenomenon.[41] The networks showed the crash of plane into tower and the collapse of the towers on a seemingly endless loop for several days, and then stopped showing them. As the signature image of the event, the crumbling, imploding towers were necessarily the locus of ambivalent and complex investments: the iconic, enticing, overenticing, and ever so slightly phobic objects of visual and televisual desire.[42] That decorum should be felt as a pressing problem in a commercial culture may seem strange, Sontag notes, "but it makes sense if understood as obscuring a host of concerns and anxieties about public order and public morale that cannot be named, as well as pointing to the inability otherwise to formulate or defend traditional conventions of how to mourn. What can be shown, what should not be shown—few issues arouse more public clamor."[43]

4. THE GIGANTIC

Elsewhere I have argued that "the aesthetic" names a stress point in Western modernity: a discursive and institutional knot where signifying mechanism and ideological investment conspire and interfere with each other in complex, unstable ways.[44] In the present context, the co-implication of aesthetic and tele-techno-mediatic problems and practices becomes visible as the twin (and twinned) problem of the aesthetic rendering of catastrophe ("after Auschwitz to write poetry is barbaric"), on the one hand, and the technical recording of

it ("Have you no human decency?"), on the other.[45] Both are sensed
to be at once necessary and violent, imperative and obscene activities.
And the violence is complex: the simile "like a movie" signifies arti-
fice and aesthetic distance (as noted earlier, it implies a certain distance—the distance of a mediation), yet also the collapse or rupture
of distance (in being not a movie but *like* one, this "event" is something else, something unnameable except by figure: a monstrously
real virtuality).

In such a context, art is never close or distant enough. It was
predictable that efforts to make art out of 9/11 would generate
spasms of outrage.[46] It was also predictable that, in the aftermath of
the attacks, the quotes from European intellectual provocateurs that
middle-highbrow American critics would most love to savor and
hate would be aestheticizing tags: Karlheinz Stockhausen, widely
quoted as saying that the attacks were "the greatest work of art that
has ever been," or Jean Baudrillard, asserting that "the horror for
the 4,000 [sic] victims of dying in those towers was inseparable from
the horror of living in them."[47] These remarks can doubtless be rendered less callous if one returns them to their contexts, but what is
of interest is the alacrity with which such *boutades* were consumed
as detachable and delectable sound bites. They allowed critics to register and disavow the aesthetic force of those haunting, endlessly
repeatable images of the towers burning and collapsing—a force that
has to do with the unstable status of the aesthetic itself. It will always
be possible to insist, as Frank Lentricchia and Jody McAuliffe do in
their rather brave gloss of Stockhausen's purported comment, that
"the suicide terrorists who struck New York may be said to have
made—with the cooperation of American television—performance
art with political designs on its American audience"—not, of course,
because the terrorists intended or the victims experienced anything
of the sort, but rather because the enormously unstable notion of
"art" in Western modernity includes a drive to negate itself *as* art so
as to "transgress and transform" society, as Lentricchia and Mc-
Auliffe put it, by communicating "the real itself."[48] The problem of
postromantic art thus ironically doubles that of testamentary technological practices (e.g., documentary photography, on-site reporting,
or other acts of witnessing), insofar as art names an effort to capture

and even *produce* the real.[49] The mass killings of 9/11 were not "art," but "art" cannot be kept at a proper and secure distance from this atrocity, any more than "the media" can.[50]

Indeed, at certain points in its development over the course of the eighteenth century, modern aesthetic theory presented itself quite overtly as a discourse of shock and of shock absorption. We tend to associate this aspect of aesthetics with theories of the sublime, but in Neoplatonic thought the beautiful arrives as a "delightful shock," and as the beautiful became a psychological experience in eighteenth-century aesthetics, it became all the more firmly associated with surprise.[51] Edmund Burke's physiological-empiricist aesthetic is particularly emphatic: *both* the sublime and the beautiful belong to a category of impression that "strikes us without any preparation"; such experiences, "seizing upon the senses and imagination, captivate the soul before the understanding is ready either to join with them or oppose them."[52] On this account, aesthetic and traumatic experience, however different from each other—and surely no difference could or should be more absolute—nonetheless suffer an odd proximity, a lingering contamination. Devoid of this trace of a wound, this hesitant openness to otherness, the beautiful becomes kitsch (and it will always, in modernity, threaten to become kitsch: these differences are constitutively unstable). The greatest twentieth-century champion of this theme was surely Adorno, whose aesthetic writings constantly emphasize the proximity of art to archaic terror: "Nietzsche's dictum that all good things were once dreadful things, like Schelling's insight into the terror of the beginning, may well have had their origins in the experience of art."[53] In this respect the sublime, about which so much has been written in conjunction with "the postmodern condition," is exemplary of a general character of the aesthetic; one could say that it exaggerates and thematizes the jolt—in Wordsworth's famous phrasing, the shock of mild surprise—that opens the modern experience of the beautiful.[54]

It may be helpful at this point briefly to invoke the tradition of the sublime with an eye to the spectacle of 9/11, since theories of the sublime describe the ambivalent pleasures of parrying this sort of wide-screen-format shock. It has, of course, been a commonplace since Aristotle that spectacles of pain can produce pleasure. "Pleasant it is," Lucretius writes in the famous opening of book 2 of *De rerum natura*, "when on the great sea the winds trouble the waters, to gaze from shore upon another's great tribulation; not because anyone's troubles are a voluptuous joy, but because to perceive what evils you are free from yourself is pleasant." Enlightenment-era theories of the sublime set out to explain the moral and psychological economies productive of that pleasure. The explanations vary considerably, of course, and it would be improper for me even to try to summarize here the history of speculation on the sublime from Boileau to Kant. Let me simply advance, as a proposition with which to begin, the more or less Burkean idea that, protected by aesthetic distance, a spectator-subject imagines surviving its own death during the sublime experience.[55] One may then add that modernity has vastly expanded this (First-World, middle-class) subject's opportunity to savor its own virtual destruction. The technological ordering and dominating of the world, Heidegger claims, brings the world before the subject as a picture or image (*Bild*).[56] The quotidian fare of violence, disaster, and death that TV audiences consume nourishes fantasies of invulnerability that grand cinematic disaster spectacles service in more richly sublime fashion. The cinematic-real-world disaster of September 11 would then represent the ne plus ultra of the sublime in and for a media society. In representing and repressing death, this aesthetic spectacle releases the theological promise of tele-vision.

The promise is a lie, of course. But the threat at work in this sort of sublime spectacle is not just that the spectators have not really been relieved of their death; it is also that, in being "like a movie," in soliciting the spectator to identify with the inhuman camera, the spectacle-transmission renders the spectator part of a process of mediation in which time and space suffer dislocation. "The world the spectacle holds up to view is at once *here* and *elsewhere*," Guy Debord writes.[57] Debord's account of the spectacle as commodity fetishism may be extended or radicalized by Derrida's vast rewriting of the Heideggerian meditation on technics and difference. The uncertain place of the image ("at once here and elsewhere") is also that of the spectator, who occupies a place opened up by iterability (the spectacle, the at-once-here-and-elsewhere, will always also be consumable elsewhere, by others). Thus the thrill of the sublime, and the more pedestrian pleasures of the televisual order generally, come laced with an irreducible anxiety. The fantasy of divine omnipotence is enabled by a more fundamental movement of dislocation and displacement.

At the end of "The Age of the World Picture," Heidegger speaks of "the gigantic" (*das Riesige*): "The gigantic presses forward . . . in the annihilation of great distances by the airplane, in the setting before us of foreign and remote worlds in their everydayness, which is produced at random through radio by a flick of the hand" (87/135). The gigantic, however, is not simply the quantitative:

> As soon as the gigantic [*das Riesige*] in planning and calculating and adjusting and making secure shifts over out of the quantitative and becomes a special quality, then what is gigantic, and what can seemingly always be calculated completely, becomes, precisely through this, incalculable. This becoming incalculable remains the invisible shadow that is cast around all things everywhere when man has been transformed into *subjectum* and the world into picture [*Bild*]. (88/135)

Heidegger risks proximity, here, to a traditional idiom of the sublime even as he seeks to move us beyond a subject-centered aesthetic. If we, in turn, accept the risk of this thought, it becomes possible to think of the spectacle of the destruction of the Twin Towers as a manifestation of the *gigantic* in this sense. That spectacle was consumed avidly, throughout the world, in affective registers that, depending on the cultural and political context, varied in their mix of horror, fascination, and elation. We have seen how this spectacle inevitably provided, and still provides, space for a sublime fantasy of invulnerability, "beyond" ground zero. But by the same token the spectacle made its impression as a major event because it made legible the "invisible shadow" of the *Riesige* as an incalculability *at the heart of the calculable*, within the very regime of technical representation through which the world becomes live feed.[58] We rediscover here, as a deconstruction of the sublime—that is to say, recast in the idiom of aesthetics—Derrida's characterization of 9/11 as an event made traumatic by a crisis of credit and a threat of the to-come that resist all representation per se.

5. *WORLD TRADE CENTER* AND *UNITED 93*

Since the attacks of September 11 inscribed a trauma in the very fabric of a culture of spectacle, big-budget films could not fail to be made about the attacks, and could not fail to be made and received nervously.[59] Both Oliver Stone's *World Trade Center* (2006) and Paul Greengrass's *United 93* (2006) seek shelter from the all too sublime, all too cinematic spectacle of 9/11 by setting their major sequences within claustrophobic spaces and by ostentatiously laying claim to a memorializing (if never quite documentary) mission. Stone's film tells the real-life story of two Port Authority officers, John Mc-Loughlin and William Jimeno, who were rescued from the rubble of the Towers, in part thanks to the vigilante efforts of a former Marine, Dave Karns (who, hearing the call of God, journeys to New York City on the night of September 11, penetrates the police perimeter, and stalks the smoking ruins, hunting for survivors). *World Trade Center*'s badly written dialogue, stereotyped gender roles, and generally retrograde politics make it an easy film to dislike, but it merits analysis as a full-bore Hollywood effort to recolonize Ground Zero. As a cinematic and cultural document, it exceeds its bellicose moral (spoken by the ex-Marine, off to reenlist as the film ends: "They're going to need some good men out there to avenge this"), its programmatic blindness to history and context (the terrorist, the source of evil, is an off-screen, satanic agent who is concretized only as the imprisoning, maiming, and killing concrete and steel of the ruined World Trade Center itself), and its pathologically fervent representations of domestic and national unity (as the rescue operation unfolds, white, black, and brown men and women find real or virtual opportunities to embrace each other). It is entirely symptomatic of the pained complexities of "September 11" that the ex-Marine—the real-life Dave Karns, who really did help rescue the men and really did reenlist afterward (he is played in the film by Michael Shannon)—should be a *fake* Marine at the time of his exploit: a civilian making illegitimate and deceptive use of his old military uniform, caught up in his role as only a wannabe can be.[60] The "like a movie" excess that the film wishes (or, better, half-wishes) to avoid returns, on the one hand, as the stylized ingredients of an "uplifting" entertainment product (the thin characterizations, the wooden dialogue, the predictable arc of a rescue narrative, the over-intense celebration of family and nation), and, on the other hand, as a slightly unstable commerce between reality and image, integrity and fakery. As the film reduces its star, Nicolas Cage, to bits of ash-covered, burned face, framed and cropped by rubble, this anticinematic movement inevitably becomes an exaggeration of the celebratory close-up of a star. On the one hand, the star's acting skills transcend his temporary defacement (the defacement, in fact, allows the star to assert himself as an artist: Cage reportedly spent hours in a sensory-deprivation tank to prepare for this role); on the other hand, the star's fragmentation registers the aggressivity with which this film turns on itself, reducing spectacle to a minimum in its most intense moments, yet always necessarily rediscovering itself as "movie."

The most dramatic and memorable shot in Stone's film transforms this ascetic movement into its complement: techno-transcendence. As the officers' underground ordeal begins, a virtual crane shot pulls out and up from hell ("We're in Hell," one trapped man says to another) to heaven—from the men buried twenty feet deep in the rubble toward the light shining down on them through a crevice in the ruin; up through the shaft of salvation, into the sky; rushing higher and higher, past Google-map's-eye view of the New York City grid and the northeast coast; coming to rest, finally, in outer space, as the camera looks down, not just like Troilus on "this litel spot of erthe" but also on a communications satellite orbiting the globe a little below the camera. From this angelic perspective we cut to representative images of a global village, united by technology and sorrow: all over the world different peoples are hearing of 9/11. (And though here as elsewhere no hint of social or political conflict is allowed representation, the specter of war looms: a glimpse of a heroic George W. Bush is followed by a clip in which a character announces to no one in particular—that is to say, to everyone: to the global, virtual community of a presumptive audience—"I don't know if anyone here knows this or not, but this country's at war."

The country would thus be at war with an enemy *beyond* the world, outside the global network of representation.)

In this sequence, *World Trade Center* encodes as a bit of virtuoso camera and computer work the vexed conspiracy between religion and tele-technology. The pressure of religious discourse has been felt repeatedly as our analysis of September 11 has unfolded—as the figures of conversion and apocalypse built into the very terms "September 11" and "Ground Zero," as the God's-eye view of history promulgated by televisual representation, and as the potentially (and traditionally) transcendent ambition of the sublime.[61] Everywhere one looks in 9/11 discourse one encounters religious motifs, from the much-circulated claim that the terrorist attacks form part of a world-historic Christian-Muslim "clash of civilizations" to the Pauline idea that "everything changed" on that day.[62] American culture is, of course, in its own peculiar way saturated with Christian practices and motifs; George W. Bush's "faith-based presidency" was an exaggeration but not really an anomaly in a postmodern world in which, as many thinkers have suggested, Western technoscientific reason and secular forms of identity both support and are supported by a monotheistic heritage.[63] *World Trade Center*'s omnipresent Christian iconography, intermittently Catholic and evangelical in flavor, manages to be at once coercive and, like Staff Sergeant Karns, slightly unhinged. When the trapped McLoughlin has a vision of his wife as a latter-day domestic non–Virgin Mary, who calls her husband back from death, we may feel that the film's bathos is calculated. But when Jimeno has a vision of Jesus bearing the water of life in an Evian bottle, it is harder to know what is intended, and with what seriousness. And when, near the beginning of the film, we meet Staff Sergeant Karns in church, staring, under a large, spare Protestant cross, at the first page of Revelation, is the film telling us that he is a knight of Christ or—or *also*—that his military-evangelical, apocalypse-ready faith has something to do with his being a whisker away from insanity? The point is not to try to gauge the degree of Stone's sense of irony but to note the persistence with which *World Trade Center* relays not just the codependency of religion and teletechnical mediation but also the fundamental tension between faith—particularly faith in the "good news" of Christ, the mediator and

Word—and the structure of iterability, of technical reproducibility (and, therefore, the inherent possibility of forgery, manipulation, loss), in and through which faith occurs. The codependent instability of faith and mediation, spectacle and unseeability, reality and virtuality, mediation and censorship, possession and loss—all the torments and paradoxes of "September 11"—find expression in the most portentous, wobbly, yet compelling line of dialogue in *World Trade Center*, spoken by the only character who could possibly speak it: the mad, damaged, former and future, but eternally ersatz Marine: "God made a curtain with the smoke to shield us from what we're not ready to see," Karns tells an awed bystander, as they stare past the camera at the occluded yet mesmerizing Twin Towers spectacle.

Greengrass's *United 93*, a shrewder and considerably more effective film than Stone's, eschews the apocalyptic idiom.[64] Even more than *World Trade Center*, this film proffers claustrophobic affect and memorializing piety as antidotes to the spectral power of the 9/11 spectacle—a spectacle that the film expels from its primary representational space, by way of some complex cinematic footwork.[65] Once the film has gotten its characters to the airport, it settles into interior spaces, cutting back and forth between the doomed airplane and the command centers of the FAA and NORAD. Greengrass, whose background includes BBC documentaries and who is well attuned to the antiaestheticism and antiprofessionalism characterizing so many structured responses to September 11, casts amateurs alongside professional actors and even has a number of characters, most notably Ben Sliney, head of the FAA command center in Herndon, Virginia, and Major James Fox at NORAD, played by their real-life selves. A number of paradoxical effects ensue. The nonprofessional actors and real-life characters give good to excellent performances—Sliney, in particular, comes as close as this film allows to being a star. (The camera returns again and again to his urban, middle-aged face as he struggles bravely and competently, though of course ineffectively, with the unfolding crisis, and he is allowed a couple of resonant lines such as "We're at war with someone.")

But nowhere does the film feel more generic than when these real people are so splendidly playing themselves. When the film cuts

away from the plane to the control centers, it becomes indistinguishable from the sort of Hollywoodesque action flick or TV drama from
which it seeks to distance itself. The film's core of power lies in its
methodical, dull, and claustrophobic representation of the beginning
of a plane flight that we know will end in death. Here, of course,
where the actors are of necessity *not* playing "themselves," all is con-
jecture and fiction except for the names of the passengers and terrorists and a few snatches of dialogue—and the quotidian reality of
commercial airflight, with which every middle-class filmgoer will be
so achingly familiar: the cluttered decor, the weary look of people in
airports in the morning, nomadic, isolated, now and then talking
into cell phones. Greengrass achieves his most chilling moments in
these early airplane scenes, as late passengers hurry to catch the
plane, sit patiently on it through take-off delays, and settle into rou-
tine as the flight gets underway: it will be a good hour into the film
before the terrorists finally strike (for we are being treated not just
to characters playing themselves when possible but to something
close to real-time drama: United 93 was attacked after it had been in
the air about forty-five minutes). Ironically, when the hijacking finally starts, the tension slackens, as once again the film slides back
into formula: huddled passengers, afraid but brave; shouting terrorists, savage but scared, two of them dressed in street-Arab-signifying
clothes (untucked white undershirts, a red bandana around the head
of the fiercest terrorist). The film is, of course, perfectly sincere in its
wish to honor the courageous resistance of the United 93 passengers,
and the jar and slip of the handheld camera and the sudden blackout
at the end of the film, as the plane crashes, are tokens of a desire
for an antitheatrical, antisublime, and above all anti-"Hollywood"
literalism: a literalism that, in its necessary failure—for of course
the film knows it cannot reproduce the suffering and death being
represented—seeks to become the sign of memorial authenticity.
(Thus the blackout at the end becomes a title card: "Dedicated to the
memory of all those who lost their lives on September 11, 2001."[66])

United 93 is cinematically at its most complex as it records the
World Trade Center attacks. We first "see" American flight 11's
crash into the north tower as the disappearance of a radar blip on an

FAA screen; moments later, via a point of view shot through binoculars held by a Newark traffic controller, we see a smoking tower, which then reappears on a TV screen. After a cut to flight 93, where the seatbelt sign has gone off but nothing yet has happened, the film returns to the FAA command center in Virginia, where the traffic controllers are realizing that United 175, "dropping like a manhole cover," is headed for New York. The command center loses track of United 175; we cut to Newark Tower, where traffic controllers pick up the plane and then see it visually, as, briefly, we do, in the digitally rendered "real world" of the movie, racing toward the south tower. But at the moment of impact what we see is a full-screen representation of the screen of a television tuned to CNN—and when the camera pulls back, we are among the stunned observers at NORAD, who are staring at their television. *United 93* stages here a canny refusal of any illusion of unmediated vision. No doubt a certain piety can be discerned in this gesture, but just as Greengrass's casting of real people as themselves produces, in the name of authenticity, a yet more bizarre concatenation of the real and the virtual, so the pious preservation of the WTC attacks as televisual images reinforces the uncanny sense of September 11 as a strangely and essentially *mediated* wound.

6. VIRTUAL TRAUMA AND TRUE MOURNING

"To speak of reality becoming a spectacle is a breathtaking provincialism," Sontag warns.[67] And surely she is right—especially if, as she goes on to claim, the postmodern, all too French theorists of the *societé du spectacle* whom she has in mind (she means Baudrillard in particular) really are guilty of suggesting "that there is no real suffering in the world" because "everyone is a spectator."[68] As Derrida (the French theorist I am most concerned to honor here) passionately reminded readers in the early 1990s, "never before, in absolute figures, never have so many men, women, and children been subjugated, starved, or exterminated on the earth."[69] Given ever-rising population levels and the ghastly inequities of the present global order, his claim remains in force and is likely to remain so for years to come. Never before in history has there been, quantitatively speaking, so much real suffering in the world. And very little of it, of course, gets taken up as mass-mediated spectacle. The images that flow in endlessly from the corners of the earth represent a tiny fraction of representable horror, and of those images only a few obtain their transient moment on television screens. Sometimes the winnowing process displays a sharply political intent; more often it relays the brutal priorities and indifferences of capital flow, ideological investment, and corporate-media practices and calculations—the last being generally, though by no means perfectly, in sync with governmental and military interests. The content, format, ideological slant, and mode of institutional production of the "news" varies considerably throughout the world, but always and everywhere it is a fact that reality only sometimes, under certain conditions, becomes spectacle. This truism is, if anything, all the more true in an era of mechanical, digital, and virtual reproducibility, even as the technologies of surveillance, inscription and transmission grow ever more powerful and profuse.

The September 11 attacks were a reality that *had to* become spectacle. This act of terrorism may have been animated by certain relatively specific political intentions, but in destroying the symbolic center of world trade it jolted a "world order" sustained by "the *credit* of American power," to recall once more Derrida's analysis.[70] This world order is, among other things, a regime of tele-technological representation: a multilayered constellation of institutions, technologies, and practices through which mediatized phenomena come to varying degrees of visibility for many heterogeneous audiences, the whole dominated, unevenly but pervasively, by American commercial, financial, political, cultural, military, and linguistic power. This world order was not affected in any simple way by the September 11 attacks. It is always hard to measure the "consequences" of a particular event in a complex system (clearly any historian seeking to get from 9/11 to the American invasion of Iraq will have a considerable array of over- and under-determinations to ponder), but certainly at present writing the global system underwriting the global diffusion of the attacks in 2001 can only be said to have been wounded if one is willing to countenance the possibility of *virtual* trauma: of a wound that, in a sense I have been trying to specify here, excceds the difference between the real and the unreal. Derrida rightly put stress on the way in which the attacks, in their precision, were traumatic insofar as they threatened a worse to come. If such violence could be suffered in New York and at the Pentagon, worse could happen again and anywhere else—even (which is to say, according to the phantasmatic logic driving the "war on terror," *above all*) in those privileged places where public disaster is *supposed* to be real only as spectacle. The true force of the attacks resides in their having happened and having also, additionally, not yet happened elsewhere. That temporal complexity is arguably proper to traumatic experience. But as we have seen, "September 11" is at once traumatic and not quite properly so: it is always also a warding off of trauma, precisely to the extent that its temporal complexity and spatial diffusion depend upon its global tele-technical diffusion as name ("September 11") and as spectacle. Here the virtuality of the trauma may be unpacked by way of another sort of paradox. On the one hand, from the point of view of the communications business, the attacks were not wounding at all; quite the reverse (if a "reverse" of wounding can be imagined): they allowed the communications business to imagine itself whole, redeemed, at one with itself. ("There was no terror or confusion at the Associated Press. There was, instead, that feeling of history being manufactured . . . 'the wonderful calm that comes into play when people are really doing their jobs'"; Junod, "Falling Man"). The attacks were grist to the mass-media mill, the show that had to be shown, repeatedly and worldwide. "September 11" was the quintessence of news. As is often remarked, these terrorists, who trained in America, used American technology to produce an American-movie-like spectacle for American TV crews, etc., were inextricably part of a system that they were turning against itself (terrorism being essentially a communicative act, they were, among other things, using the American-dominated global communications network to reach real and imagined Muslim audiences). And this also means that, although, on the one hand, the September 11 attacks were the epitome of Western news, on the other hand, the very fact that they *had* to be shown conveyed a subtle threat—registered a virtual trauma. The system of accreditation *had* to expose itself as (virtually) vulnerable, open to an unpredictable future. The news being transmitted from America under the hypermnemic, hyperforgetful sign of the name-date was therefore not just that this event was virtual because, as the promise of its own repetition, it had not yet fully arrived but also that it was virtual in its needing to be transmitted. Because it happened at the center, the symbolic center of the global-televisual "here," it must be re- and decentered by being broadcast everywhere, and everywhere received as a destruction of a "here" that is not the spectator's—except virtually. That spectacle both wounds (in marking the finitude of the accrediting system and recording the displacing power of modern technics) and disavows the wound (it happened elsewhere, precisely *as* spectacle). Spectacle here, in other words, both screens and relays "something worse" beyond "the archaic theater of violence aimed at striking the imagination."[71] Heidegger's figure of the "gigantic," as we saw, gestures toward this element of incalculability and invisibility; if we want less proximity to the idiom of the sublime, the figure of the "virtual," suggestive as it is of a trembling on the edge of presence, is perhaps to be preferred.

This dissolve of the event into its mediation, its dis-placement, is what drives commentary on 9/11 to such fantastic excess (the present effort being no exception). In its most hermeneutically primitive form, this excess manifests itself as simple repudiation: the spectrality of the event becomes a clash of civilizations, a war of monotheisms, or, even more primitively, a para-religious struggle between good and evil, where evil is first abstracted as "terror" and then personified and given a face (Osama, Saddam). A paranoid twist on this binary schematizing produces conspiracy theory: here the U.S. government becomes its own other and either passively (the LIHOP version: "let it happen on purpose") or aggressively (MIHOP: "make it happen on purpose") attacks itself. The photos and video recordings in the archive now become texts to be pored over rather than simply pointed to; every shadow or puff of smoke is analyzed—yet only in order to rediscover, once again, a single meaning and an us versus them ethical structure (the "us" now being the interpreters, standing in for the People, against a renegade government).

More sophisticated readings, attentive to the spectral force of "September 11," reproduce the excess of the event as a more self-involved interpretive madness. Baudrillard's provocative interpretations have a manifestly oneiric quality to them ("we have dreamt of this event . . . they *did it*, but we *wished for* it"), and his close reading of the Twin Towers as architectural text (which brilliantly glosses their twinness as "the embodiment of a system that is no longer competitive, but digital and countable, and from which competition has disappeared in favor of networks and monopoly") slides in and out of dreamlike personifications: "When the two towers collapsed, you had the impression that they were responding to the suicides of the suicide-planes with their own suicides."[72] Baudrillard, in short, transforms spectrality into theological self-referentiality, thereby remaining well within the haunted, defensive loopings of 9/11 discourse: "It has been said that 'Even God cannot declare war on Himself.' Well, He can. The West, in the position of God (divine omnipotence and absolute moral legitimacy), has become suicidal, and declared war on itself."[73] Such formulations recirculate the figure of a sovereign, imperial subject, suicidal in its narcissism (for the story of Narcissus is above all a suicide story), theological in its guiding coordinates: this suicidal subject is the subject of an ontotheological tradition that has arguably never been stronger or more capable of laying waste to the world. Yet such formulations also record the pressure of a haunting irreducible to self and other, and other as self. "Autoimmunity" was one of the terms Derrida mobilized in his late work to suggest the phantasmatic nature of all selves (not least a self called "the West") and to stress a "quasi-suicidal" movement at work in all processes of identification and technologization.[74] On this account, if the atrocity of 9/11 drew on the representational codes of American disaster movies and more generally on American and Western technological resources, on American Cold War political activity in Afghanistan, etc., we do better to speak not of a subject's dreaming its own death but of a death at work, doubly, silently, irrevocably, in all symbolic orders, all movements of capitalization and technologization. Not that 9/11 was inevitable: rather, as trauma, it recorded the impact of death as the unforeseeable and unimaginable, and it did so, paradoxically, all the more powerfully *because* it repeated so uncannily the codes of mass-mediated spectacle. The sense that finitude, incalculability, and difference underwrite the commodified technospectacle of the everyday is precisely what makes the spectacle of 9/11 into virtual trauma.

We have seen how the name-date "September 11" and the toponym "Ground Zero" draw their fetishistic energies from this fundamental ambivalence. Both terms move beyond themselves, as it were, and in a double sense: on the one hand, by emphasizing survival and encouraging all the phantasms of power—of picturing, targeting, naming, annihilating, and consuming—that drive the "war on terror"; on the other hand, by surreptitiously exploiting an iterability and finitude conditioning of all life, technology, and mourning. We have traced the double, ambivalent movement of moving beyond in various registers: as the name-date, which obtains rhetorical power only by half-confessing its openness to citation and loss; as the discourse of targeting; as the simultaneously narcissistic and dislocating activity of spectating; and as the seductions and uncertainties of aesthetic spectacle, mediation, and tele-technology. The more the world superpower dials the 9–1-1 emergency number, gives a name and a face to evil and goes to war, the more haunting September 11 becomes. Overwritten by atrocity after atrocity committed in its name, its afterimage persists. As a hypermnemic name-date, it whisperingly confirms its forgettability even as it calls upon us to remember.

True mourning, if we achieve it, listens to this whisper while remembering and endures patiently the finitude and exhaustion that make memory possible. "Images shown on television are by definition images of which, sooner or later, one tires," Sontag writes (105). But in a surprising move near the end of *Regarding the Pain of Others*, and to some extent brushing against the grain of her own previous work, she insists on the moral imperative to affirm rather than lament the glut of images. "That we are not totally transformed, that we can turn away, turn the page, switch the channel, does not impugn the ethical value of an assault by images. It is not a defect that we are not seared, that we do not suffer *enough*, when we see these images" (116–17). Turning away both from the idiom of conversion and from the long Western tradition of identifying media overstimulation with ethically numbing shock, Sontag emphasizes the modest yet infinite task of receiving and thinking. "Such images cannot be more than an invitation to pay attention, to reflect, to learn, to examine the rationalizations for mass suffering offered by established powers" (117). Such images do not speak for themselves: no image does. They must be read; they call on us to read them because they represent the effaced singularity of a life lived, a death suffered. They relay the claim made on us by the nameless and faceless dead. Through all its hallucinatory reinvocations and vicissitudes, the name "September 11" relays that finite but morally absolute claim.

PART II

War on Terror

The aide said that guys like me were "in what we call the reality-based community," which he defined as people who "believe that solutions emerge from your judicious study of discernible reality." I nodded and murmured something about enlightenment principles and empiricism. He cut me off. "That's not the way the world really works anymore," he continued. "We're an empire now, and when we act, we create our own reality. And while you're studying that reality—judiciously, as you will—we'll act again, creating other new realities, which you can study too, and that's how things will sort out. We're history's actors . . . and you, all of you, will be left to just study what we do."

—RON SUSKIND, "Faith, Certainty, and the Presidency of George W. Bush," *The New York Times Magazine* (October 17, 2004)

WHO SPEAKS, and in what mode, when war is declared on terror? What are the conditions of possibility for this speech act; what clumps of historical context cling to it? To what performative felicity could it aspire? Has such a declaration of war indeed ever occurred; could it ever occur or, for that matter, not occur? Since September 11, 2001, the world has been enduring the consequences of what the global media declares—sometimes skeptically, and often disapprovingly—to be a war declared by the United States on terror, yet in many ways it is hard to imagine a speech act more peculiar than this declaration. In this chapter I risk (risk and rhetorical overkill being inseparable from this topic) the extravagant claim that the declaration of war on terror is *the* exemplary speech act of sovereignty for our era, which is also to say that it comes into being as a conflicted, excessive performative—a phantasmatic speech act nearly as intoxicated as the dream of godlike sovereignty that the Bush administration aide is entertaining in Ron Suskind's well-known article. Only an American president, a puissant pseudo-sovereign in an era of multinational capitalism and technomediation, could have declared such a war—if, in fact, it has been declared at all, or even exists at all, except as a symptom, a phantasmatic discharge, cast up in response to what I have called the "virtual trauma" of the September 11 attacks but referring back in more diffuse and uncertain fashion to wider, less stable contexts: to the variously military, economic, technical, semiotic, and ideological forms of domination that we summarize sometimes as Western imperialism and sometimes as globalization; to the career of modern political and ideological debate since the French Revolution; even, in indirect and massively mediated fashion, to modes of ontological and epistemological uncertainty that we sometimes trope as "language," celebrate as "literature," or (in certain quarters) castigate as "theory."

1. THE SOVEREIGN AND THE TERRORIST

Let me begin again, asking (and to some extent answering) a somewhat simpler and more specific version of my opening question: Did the United States ever declare war on terror? In one sense, no, of course: the United States has not issued a formal declaration of war since the Second World War. Indeed, according to Bob Woodward's account of the Bush administration's response to the September 11 attacks, the president specified, in a meeting with congressional leaders on September 12, 2001, that "he did not want a declaration of war from the Congress but would be interested in a resolution endorsing the use of force."[1] Yet in Woodward's book, as in the Western media at large, a certain "declaration" nonetheless declares itself. Here is Woodward describing the president hearing the news of the World Trade Center attacks, a few minutes after the second plane hit:

> A photo of that moment is etched for history. The president's hands are folded formally in his lap, his head turned to hear [the chief of staff's] words. His face has a distant sober look, almost frozen, edging on bewilderment. Bush remembers exactly what he was thinking: "They had declared war on us, and I made up my mind at that moment that we were going to war." (15)

Michael Moore's mercilessly extended close-up of this distant, "almost frozen," bewildered presidential face in *Fahrenheit 911* no doubt offers us a more satisfying portrait than Woodward's prose does, but the latter's Gothic figures of etching and freezing suggest nicely, after their fashion, the ambiguity of sovereign power at the

moment of the declaration of war on terror. It is only here, in Bush's
retrospective dramatization of a bit of his internal life to a journalist,
that a declaration of war occurs—or, more precisely, has *already* occurred: "They had declared war on us." It is the other, the terrorist,
who declares war; the president, in the staged immediacy of his interior consciousness, merely declares war back: "I made up my mind
at that moment that we were going to war." This mingling of reac-
tive and proactive rhetoric, characteristic of most of the administration's pronouncements about the war on terror, was to feature largely
in Bush's State of the Union Address of January 20, 2004 ("America
is on the offensive against the terrorists who started this war. . . . The
terrorists and their supporters declared war on the United States, and
war is what they got"). War as declaration originates elsewhere: the
wielder of sovereign power, playing, as it were, a fort-da game with
himself (and if only for this reason I shall gender the sovereign male
in what follows), relegates sovereignty to the other in order to take
it back. The true performativity of war as declaration is thus imagined to take place at a distance, and the sovereign speech act thereby
becomes tinged with constative responsibility. Bush's decisive but re-
active act ("I made up my mind at that moment") subordinates sovereign freedom to factual context: the performative utterance will
also be a referentially stable description of a preexistent condition.
(And in fact, the ambiguously performative and constative utterance
"We're at war" seems to have been, if Woodward can be trusted,
one of Bush's first articulate recorded sentences in the wake of the
attacks.)[2]

The double gesture through which sovereign power is given away
so as to be more securely reclaimed is, of course, a ruse. Would a true
sovereign, as opposed to a U.S. president, have need of it? Perhaps
not, though the concept of sovereignty has such a complicated genealogy and structure that we might wish to leave the question open.
Sovereignty, "the absolute and perpetual power of a commonwealth," to cite Jean Bodin's definition, is above the law but never
lawless: "if we say that to have absolute power is not to be subject to
any law at all, no prince of this world will be sovereign, since every
earthly prince is subject to the laws of God and of nature and to

various human laws that are common to all peoples."[3] In this tradition even the absolute monarch must ultimately be defined by his
limitations, his sovereign right to go to war haunted by the question
of whether his war is *just*.[4] The medieval conception of just war and
the early modern theorization of sovereignty as supreme authority
within a territory compound uneasily even in the so-called age of
absolutism, let alone the era of the rights of man, technical reproducibility, and global capitalism. If, as Jean-Luc Nancy claims, war is
"the *technē*, the *art*, *execution*, or *operation* [mise en oeuvre] of Sovereignty itself," one may hypothesize that war, the supreme expression
of sovereignty, is also—therefore—the locus of sovereignty's strategic
and momentary, but perhaps also symptomatic, self-occlusion.[5] Has
any Leviathan within this postmedieval Western context ever failed
to plead the necessity of his acts of violence? ever simply declared
war as a declaration of his own utterly unfettered desire? Possibly
so, but given the striking frequency with which sovereign powers
displace responsibility for war onto their adversaries, I want to postu-
late in the following pages that at the heart of modernity's rudimen-
tarily secularized idea of sovereignty lies *terror*: a terror proper to
sovereignty itself; in a sense a terror *of* itself—of a performativity
intrinsic to yet in some way resistant to sovereignty, resistant at least
to sovereignty understood as the indivisibility or presence-to-self of
an act of will.

Of course, a U.S. president is not, speaking at all properly, a "sovereign." As the elected leader of a republic, he has limited powers
within the polity, and even those powers are vulnerable to counter-
pressure and compromise. Yet as the executive officer of the world's
superpower, a U.S. president may nonetheless be said to stand in
more proximate (if also more vexed) relation to sovereignty than
any of the contemporary world's various dictators and tyrants. Many
rulers, to be sure, rule their states far more obviously than a U.S.
president rules the United States—indeed, a U.S. president, produced and defined as he is not just by constitutional provisions but
by the strictures of a vast corporate, bureaucratic, and financial order,
cannot be said to "rule" his country at all. Such is the general deep-
structure condition of modern power, if we credit Michel Foucault's

account of the eclipse of early modern sovereignty in favor of late modern "governmentality." ("Governmentality," in Judith Butler's helpful formulation, "is broadly understood as a mode of power concerned with the maintenance and control of bodies and persons. . . . Marked by a diffuse set of strategies and tactics, governmentality gains its meaning and purpose from no single source, no unified sovereign subject."[6]) A concept like governmentality describes well the workings of power in advanced capitalist societies.

Yet sovereignty not only persists as a fundamental principle of international law and politics but also remains, as various critics (Butler included) have argued, a concept descriptive of paralegal deployments of power throughout the global order. And if we ask after the fate and nature of sovereignty in our era—the age of global capital, population management, technical deracination, nuclear threat—at some point we cannot help recasting the question as one about "America," the nation that sustains, however ambivalently, the "prevailing world order" with the "credit" of its military, economic, and cultural power.[7] So let me hypothesize that we glimpse the anxious endoskeleton of postmodern sovereign power when we examine Bush's reaction to the September 11 attacks. The panic, touched on by Woodward and relished by Moore, that freezes Bush's face as he absorbs the news of the attacks no doubt has something to tell us about Bush himself—about the swagger, hysteria, and incompetence characteristic of this particular man, playing this particular public role—but it may also be taken as a little allegory of sovereignty's relation to terror.[8] The violent act through which war—war and terror, war as terror—enters the world is always declared to be prior and elsewhere, the fault of the other. The sovereign will no doubt claim the right to "preemptive" violence—but not a whit more. In advance, the "preemptive" strike names itself as secondary, for it is the sovereign's claim that sovereign terror arises in response to the initial, instituting, genuinely *performative* terror of the terrorist. This peculiar wrinkle in sovereignty—this ambivalent abnegation of institutive force, or of what Walter Benjamin would call law-positing violence (*rechtsetzende Gewalt*)—characterizes in our era not just the sovereign's relation to war but also that of his opponent, the enemy named "terrorist."[9] According to the narrative that surfaces as soon as the "terrorist" is being brought (however briefly) within the orbit of the understandable, terrorists go to their martyrdom in response to previous acts of violence: "America and its allies" are from this perspective the true "international terrorists."[10] In short: war, as terror, has always already been started by the other, the terrorist. Under such circumstances, sovereign is he who decides on terror—who can call the other a terrorist and make it stick.[11]

The declaration of war on terror respects and exaggerates the complications of conventional declarations of war and gives them an extra twist. If all war requires an enemy, the war on terror, as its critics have so often pointed out, declares itself waged against a globalized, absolute enemy. A concatenation of historical events and trends, ranging from the immediate wound of the September 11 attacks to the vast tissue of twentieth-century and especially post–Cold War global politics—and ultimately to the deep-time historical fashioning of Europe and the "West"—ensures that this enemy will be Islamic. But at least in principle the enemy faces and names are temporary, and the war, having no object except the abstraction "terrorism" or "terror," is limitless and endless. The theater of this conflict is the earth itself, including, of course, the "homeland," plus any portion of outer space that can be militarized. The war on terror is thus an *absolute* declaration of war: the declaration of an absolute war, an absolutely total war. Its religious character is therefore irreducible. The ideological and political ties between the Bush administration and evangelical Christian groups are obviously of significance here, but the war on terror has a deeper theological root system than either the personal beliefs of a particular president or the power play of factional U.S. politics can account for. In the early days after the September 11 attacks, the administration's theological allusions were particularly marked, though usually later provisionally disowned ("this crusade, this war on terror"; "Operation Infinite Justice"; "an axis of evil"). Stress also fell on the war on terror's exceptional character. This war was to be fought "in the shadows" (Dick Cheney). It was to be "a new kind of war . . . political, economic, diplomatic, military. It will be unconventional, what we do" (Donald Rumsfeld). "Americans should not expect one battle but a lengthy campaign, unlike any other we have ever seen. It may include dramatic strikes visible on TV, and covert operations, secret even in success" (George W. Bush).[12] New, unconventional, even at times—like the futuristic warfare imagined by Benjamin—imperceptible, this war was to surpass all limit, all law, all representational convention or mediation.[13] The declaration of war on terror declares war *as* terror.

Yet this war is undecidably a war and a "war." Its infinite, absolute seriousness and contagiousness (who or what could oppose a war on terror?) has about it an unbearable lightness, even, for all the suffering it causes and damage it does, a certain silliness, for a war without limits transforms its very prosecution into a sequence of theatrically ineffective gestures. To be sure, this "declaration of war" has had effects as massive as any sovereign speech act could hope to have: it cleared a political path for the array of crimes against international law and human rights for which the Bush administration has become famous; it has been invoked by judges in U.S. courtrooms to justify detentions, the nondisclosure of evidence, etc.; in its name the United States has mounted two massive invasions and spent well over half a trillion dollars. And certainly, at present writing, the war in Iraq is as bloody and real as any war ever was. But all of this has not prevented the "war on terror" from seeming perpetually ready to melt into air. It is a war declared—and undeclared and semi-declared—by an executive officer whose words in many contexts carry enormous force but whose powers (unlike those of the U.S. Congress) do not (quite) include the legal power to declare war.[14] Its beginning is nearly as uncertain as its end: it scrolls back past the September 11 attacks and the Bush administration's pronouncements, even past the 1993 attack on the World Trade Center, to incorporate into its history other attacks, other administrations, other nations.[15] It is uncertainly literal and figurative; it forces ponderous legal documents to pause in mid-stride to muddle out—I quote here from a brief submitted to the Supreme Court in 2004— whether "the United States is actually 'at war' in the sense of Vietnam, Korea, and the two World Wars rather than in the sense of the 'war on drugs,' which is, and always has been, primarily a law enforcement effort."[16] The war's very existence seems questionable, as the war-on-terror president himself at least once conceded during his eight years in office. ("I know that some people question if America is really in a war at all," Bush remarked in his 2004 State of the Union speech.) After all, if the war is so absolute as to be at times invisible, how can one tell whether it is going on or not? Where is it to be found, either in the "homeland," where consumers are being exhorted to consume more, or in the areas of the world (or, for that matter, sectors of U.S. society) where direct and semi-direct applications of American power have been part of reality for a half-century or more? Even granted that the Bush administration may well be the most ideologically driven administration in modern U.S. history, has its neoconservative ideology produced an imperialism different in its fundamentals from that of previous administrations?[17] That in the wake of the September 11 attacks the United States launched visible police, military, and paramilitary actions against certain terrorist groups and attacked Afghanistan and Iraq, that within the United States we have witnessed displays of warlike behavior—the aggressive recruitment of young working-class men to feed the military machine; the programmatic harassment of "Arabs," Muslims, foreigners, and certain sorts of citizens; the semi-legalization of torture and interminable incarceration; in short, a general deterioration and at times ghastly violation of human rights and civil liberties—all this does not add up clearly to "war on terror," because no act short of nuclear apocalypse could in the end be adequate to such a war. The choreographing of fear and the militarization of public life in the United States will thus at times seem absurd or stagy (as in the case of the much-mocked color-coded terror alerts), while conventional military operations against other sovereign states will always risk being seen, even by ardent interventionists, as surrogates for the "real" war on terror. Baudrillard might well tell us, and not entirely without reason, that the war on terror does not exist—or, more precisely, does not *take place*. It goes on, perhaps, but it does not (quite) take place, as a determinate event within a determinate space and time.

The declaration of war on terror is undecidably and incalculably performative and constative, real and fictional, literal and rhetorical, consequent and nugatory, radically singular and endlessly iterable and generalizable. On the one hand, it can seem "in a peculiar way hollow or void," as J. L. Austin famously characterized literary utterances.[18] On the other hand, its consequences—legal, political, economic—can seem as traceable as those of any performative. "Declaring" "war," the pseudo-sovereign becomes a little more sovereign, in and through his own flawed, quasi-fictional exercise of sovereignty.[19] This exceptional declaration of war thus exemplifies the sort of performative that J. Hillis Miller has taught us to understand as "literary"—literary here signaling not (as Austin would have it) a performative safely framed and tagged as fictional but rather a performative that troubles the difference between real and fictional, literal and figurative. Speech act theory, Miller suggests, is a speech act that exceeds its own theory of itself. It unfolds as a contradiction (relying on a speaker's intention, but subordinating intention to context); it depends on the "parasitic," "nonserious" literary examples it excludes. Like a sovereign declaring war on terror, it downplays its own performativity: Austin's *How to Do Things with Words* "is a truly revolutionary philosophical event attempting to masquerade as a constative statement of fact that does no more than continue a development in thinking long underway."[20] The analogy between sovereign and text is not as forced as it might seem. Miller's analysis draws attention to the fact that a revolutionary event "definitely does not fit Austin's criteria for a felicitous performative," since it cannot rely upon preexisting laws or conventions: "A revolution is groundless, or rather, by a metaleptic future anterior, it creates the grounds that justify it" (26–27). And, commenting on the disorder and violence that so often characterize Austin's examples, Miller remarks that, in the Austinian subtext, "we are always skating on thin ice, on the verge of catastrophe" (56).[21] In Austin, as in Nietzsche, we hang in dreams from the back of a tiger, for the social order, relying as it does on congenitally unreliable performatives, can at any moment give way (which is why, Miller suggests, "a rhythmic counterpoint of multitudinous references to law, lawyers, judges, and courtroom scenes punctuates *How to Do Things with Words*"; 56). In its own way, speech act theory may be said to wage a little war on terror. And it offers a theory of why the sovereign shies away from himself: the terror at the heart of sovereignty is that of the performative itself, or rather, of the literariness—the radical uncertainty—making the performative possible.

In some ways it has always been clear that a degree of reflection on language becomes inescapable as soon as one has begun to think about sovereignty, war, and terror. For starters, the war on terror is, among other things, very much a war of words. Sovereign is he, I suggested earlier, who can make the word "terror" stick; it must be added that this Anglo-Latinate word, which has a history we shall have to examine, functions as a politically charged site of translation within a globally hegemonic English-language media apparatus. (All political conflicts consequential enough to achieve media representation necessarily involve, as part of their struggle, their translation into the Anglo-Latinate lexicon of "terror." The military, cultural, and economic dominance of the West is thus always also an ongoing act of translation that forms an integral part of the "war on terror.") Within that media apparatus, a symptomatic slippage occurs, from "terrorist" or "terrorism" to the more general "terror," whereby —we shall return to this—the "war" achieves theological stature as a war on evil—and on finitude, vulnerability, death itself. If we can speak of a terror within sovereignty, a terror that sovereignty exploits and depends on but with which it is endlessly at war, it is terror in this sense: the mark of a finitude internal to sovereignty, which is to say, a vulnerability to "language" to the extent that we understand language as an uncertain medium, productive of unpredictable effects. Counterintuitive though it may seem, a meditation on the war on terror, as noted earlier, ultimately entangles us in the seemingly academic and culturally marginal question of "literary theory" and of a certain war on theory—a war waged in the name of certainty, clarity, referential stability—that forms part of the history and constitution of theory itself, particularly within the American intellectual cultures and cultural institutions that began producing and publicizing this particular notion of "literary theory" some four decades ago—but not only there, and not only since the 1970s.[22] Theory has been blamed for terror at least since the words "terrorism" and "terrorist"—along with, I shall suggest, the first drafts of the notion of a "war on terror"—emerged during the early years of the French

Revolution. Eventually I shall track some of those developments, though first I want to spend a little more time exploring the dense, overdetermined notions of war and terror that became joined at the hip in the Bush administration's signature phrase.

2. SOVEREIGNTY AT WAR

To begin with, however, perhaps a few more words about sovereignty, as a way of getting us to war. I have been suggesting that uncertainty, and a strategic capitalization on uncertainty, haunts sovereignty; arguably this is particularly true in our technomediated era. The major shortcoming of Agamben's provocative hypothesis that "the camp is the *nomos* of modernity" is its overhasty absolutization of its own terms:

> If . . . the essence of the camp consists in the materialization of the state of exception and in the subsequent creation of a space in which bare life and the juridical rule enter into a threshold of indistinction, then we must admit that we find ourselves virtually in the presence of a camp every time such a structure is created, independent of the kinds of crime that are committed there and whatever its denomination and specific topography. The stadium in Bari into which the Italian police in 1991 provisionally herded all illegal Albanian immigrants before sending them back to their country, the winter cycle-racing track in which the Vichy authorities gathered the Jews before consigning them to the Germans, the *Konzentrationslager für Ausländer* in Cottbus-Sielow in which the Weimar government gathered Jewish refugees from the East, or the *zones d'attentes* in French international airports in which foreigners asking for refugee status are detained will then all equally be camps. In all these cases, an apparently innocuous space (for example, the Hôtel Arcades in Roissy) actually delimits a space in which the normal order is de facto suspended and in which whether or not atrocities are committed depends not on law but on the civility and ethical sense of the police who temporarily act as sovereign (for example, in the four days during which foreigners can be held in the *zone d'attente* before the intervention of the judicial authority).[23]

Borrowing heavily (and, it must be said, not always with copious acknowledgment) from Hannah Arendt, Agamben draws attention to the twentieth-century proliferation of "camps" throughout civic space and suggests that the camp, as the space of an "absolute impossibility of deciding between fact and law, rule and application, exception and rule" (173), provides "the hidden matrix of the politics in which we are still living" (175).[24] His argument is in many ways persuasive, but it needs to be qualified on at least two points: first, *there is no such thing as an absolute camp*—even Auschwitz was exposed to systems and pressures larger than itself—and, second, there is, therefore, no single, homogeneous space called "camp" to which the various examples listed in the quotation above can be assimilated without residue. It is simply not the case that "everything is possible" in a *zone d'attente* in the same way that (almost) everything was possible in the Nazi extermination camps or the killing fields of Cambodia or Rwanda. (Nor are these acts and sites of genocide interchangeable or equivalent in the way in which they made "everything possible.") The claim that in a late-twentieth-century European refugee camp the police "temporarily act as sovereign" is valid, but only and precisely to the extent that one understands sovereign power as fractured, contaminated, and mediated—paradoxically so. "A pure sovereignty is indivisible or it is not at all," Derrida writes. Yet in order to be indivisible—in order to be the pure instantaneity of the exceptional decision—sovereignty must withdraw from time and language:

> To confer sense or meaning on sovereignty, to justify it, to find a reason for it, is already to compromise its deciding exceptionality, to subject it to rules, to a code of law, to some general law, to concepts. It is thus to divide it, to subject it to partitioning, to participation, to being shared. It is to take into account the part played by sovereignty. And to take that part or share into account is to turn sovereignty against itself, to compromise its immunity. This happens as soon as one speaks of it in order to give it or find in it some sense or meaning. But since this happens all the time, pure sovereignty does not exist; it is always in the process of positing itself by refuting itself, by denying or disavowing itself; it is always in the process of autoimmunizing itself.[25]

This ontological predicament, offered by Derrida as a general condition of sovereignty, takes a more specific historical form as the paradox of an American "war on terror" driven to exploit contingent and unstable zones of ambiguity within the sovereign-territorial economy of the global order.[26] The struggle within the U.S. courts and between the executive and judicial arms of the U.S. government over the legal status of the Guantánamo prison camp illustrates the paradox nicely: under current conditions, the world superpower can generate a state of exception most easily in spaces to which it does not lay proper sovereign claim. Guantánamo, which, with Abu Ghraib, is thus far the twenty-first century's most notorious locus of sovereign exception—a space in which guards, petty officials, interrogators, secret service agents, independent contractors, and ultimately the entire executive arm of the U.S. government "act as sovereign"—was produced as a space of exception in the shadow of sovereign ambiguity (nominally under the sovereignty of Cuba, Guantánamo is "leased" to the United States in perpetuity), and this camp proved vulnerable to Supreme Court review precisely to the extent that the court was willing to limit the ambiguity on which sovereign exceptionality was relying—finding, in the words of the majority opinion authored by Justice Stevens in *Rasul et al. v. Bush* (2004), that writ of habeas corpus applies in "a territory over which the United States exercises plenary and exclusive jurisdiction, but not 'ultimate sovereignty.' "[27] The sovereign claim to exception was absolute, as always—the Bush administration's position was that the court had no business reviewing the case at all—but was checked in this instance by the court's own ("sovereign") decision provisionally to integrate Guantánamo into the polity's rule of law. By simply deciding to hear this and subsequent cases (*Hamdan v. Rumsfeld* [2006] and, as the present study goes to press, the important *Boumediene v. Bush* [2008]) on the right of Guantánamo prisoners to habeas corpus, the court, one could say in Benjaminian terms, brought Guantánamo within the fold of law-conserving power through a law-positing speech act. These cases could easily have been decided differently, of course, or not been heard at all: the point is not that the Bush administration was bound to lose, and certainly not that prisoners in this or any other camp have, pragmatically speaking, much hope of having their cases heard within the American legal system. (Guantánamo has been far more exposed to judicial review than other camps in America's new gulag, most of which are better hidden, more mobile, or more securely secreted within the sovereign territory of a client nation, militarized zones, etc.) The general point is simply that the spaces of sovereign exception are singular, quasi-localized, vulnerable to context, and exposed to contingency; the more specific point is that the American "war on terror" has put on display the paradox of a sovereign power exercising itself most freely when the legitimacy of its sovereignty is at least symbolically compromised.[28]

Agamben is in many respects highly attentive to sovereignty's essential relation to ambiguity. Stressing, like all theorists of sovereignty from Bodin onward, sovereignty's double location "outside and inside the juridical order" (15), Agamben emphasizes that the sovereign exception opens the space of law and politics ("the rule, suspending itself, gives rise to the exception and, maintaining itself in relation to the exception, first constitutes itself as a rule"; 18), and is therefore "essentially unlocalizable" (19), a "suspension of every actual reference" (20). What Agamben seems at times to forget, however, is that this radical state of suspension exceeds its own decisive occasion: sovereignty must evade or repress the very "suspension" upon which it draws.[29] In coming into existence, the sovereign ban splits internally, doubling and resisting itself (as law-positing and law-conserving violence, performative force and constative reference: once again, we recall the sovereign's foot-shuffle as he declares war). With this proviso in mind, we may entertain Agamben's imaginative claim that the sovereign ban opens political space by producing *homo sacer*, the man who "can be killed and yet not sacrificed," whose inclusive exclusion founds the city of men. As the original biopolitical body—the originary inscription of what Agamben calls "bare life" within political life—*homo sacer* is the sovereign's inverted double (as the outlaw who can be killed without consequence by anyone, he is the man over whom all men are sovereign, whereas the sovereign is the man for whom all men are, at least potentially, *homines sacri*). Thus, according to this narrative, "the first foundation of political life is a life that may be killed, which is politicized through its very capacity to be killed" (89). Agamben offers these speculations as a meditation on the archaic root of the modern sociopolitical disposition that Foucault calls biopower (or, with a difference in emphasis, "governmentality"). Modern biopolitics, Agamben suggests, causes "the realm of bare life" to "coincide with the political realm" from which it was originally, if uncertainly, excluded (9). As a result, in modernity the state of exception becomes the rule, and the camp becomes the matrix of political space. In other words—it is here, once again, that we have to press Agamben past some of his own formulations—sovereignty suffers and exploits ever more visibly its constitutive uncertainty, even as effects of sovereignty proliferate (as paramilitary actions, kidnappings, assassinations, camp atrocities, torture sessions, etc., performed or staffed by a mix of government, military, and private-sector agents, all acting beyond the law, yet within a gray area established and underwritten, though not always thoroughly controlled, by the highest authority). It is within this matrix that "the terrorist" becomes the pseudo-sovereign's ambivalent *homo sacer*. On the one hand, the terrorist is the sovereign's putative double as a declarer of war; on the other hand—and for precisely that reason—he is the one who can be "killed but not sacrificed," sometimes immediately (as the object of a newly rehabilitated U.S. policy of targeted assassination), sometimes indirectly (as the illegitimate "enemy combatant" who disappears into the camps).

That the United States, as the world's pseudo-sovereign, should go to "war" against the terrorist underscores the peculiar ambivalence of their mutual relationship. The last person a properly Agamben-style sovereign would go to war against would be *homo sacer*: as bare life, *homo sacer* is the sovereign's abject double, but he is not an *enemy*. He is an outlaw: he is lower than an enemy, and, being both excluded from and included within the city, he is more ambivalently situated than any enemy could be. The terrorist gives to this structure yet one more twist: he is the enemy outlaw. Possessed, like a sovereign power, of *jus belli*—the right to declare and go to war—he nonetheless (as "enemy combatant") falls below the laws of war and, unprotected by law, becomes bare life to be exterminated. "War" has become the name of this thoroughly ambivalent relationship between

sovereign and terrorist for fundamental reasons. Once terrorism becomes a globalized, deracinated, Al-Qaeda–style threat, it becomes
the phantasmatic double of global American quasi-sovereignty itself,
which, as we have seen, allows the terrorist to "declare war" on an
America that itself produces this declaration by declaring war back.
No other nation could have attempted such a literary and violently
consequential speech act without falling into mere comic posturing
(one cannot imagine even Russia or China declaring war on terror),
and no other unconventional opponent could have been set up as the
enemy of sovereignty itself, so as to achieve the quasi-sovereign status
required for the role of war-declarer (the drug lords targeted by the
U.S. "war on drugs," being pirates rather than partisans, were in this
respect very feeble precursors). Of course, ever since it was announced as such, the "war on terror" has been denounced both as a
misnomer and as a policy mistake by intelligent and worldly com-
mentators. The United States, it is often pointed out, would prose-
cute its "war" more effectively if, like Europe, it understood
terrorism to be not an act of war but a crime, a matter for the police
and the courts rather than the military and the CIA. The argument
has pragmatic appeal, but sovereignty has limited commerce with
pragmatism.[30] Not that the United States *had* to declare war on terror
in precisely the way that it did (who knows: a Gore administration
might possibly have called less strongly on the trope and trappings of
war when responding to the September 11 crisis), but the American
invocation of war was deeply overdetermined, if not inevitable. The
United States went to "war" against terrorism in 2001 because the
United States cherishes its sovereign exceptionalism, which is to say,
its dominant position within a globally interdependent, technically
deracinated, and thus fundamentally indomitable world.

War is the ultimate enactment of the sovereign exception, and
thus, as sovereignty has become more visibly fractured in the modern
era, the word "war" has proliferated all the more virulently and
become all the harder to pin down. As is well known, the very notion
of war—"an organized, legitimized, lethal conflict between human
communities," to cite one scholar's definitional effort—has become
recalcitrant over the past century, with the breakdown of the Enlightenment-era *jus publicum Europaeum*.[31] Indeed, the classic European concept of war—as a political instrument practiced by

European sovereign states, substantially if imperfectly governed by laws and norms—was a relatively brief accomplishment (its *floriat* spanning some two centuries or so, from the end of the religious wars of the seventeenth century to the First World War), which excluded non-European space from its purview (colonial wars fought against non-European peoples did not fall under the same laws and norms) and could never quite exclude either the possibility or the reality of other forms of warfare (civil war, guerrilla and partisan war, revolutionary war). Carl Schmitt thus describes the laws of European warfare as a "bracketing" of war—a temporary, limited, and perhaps in the end illusory attempt to have, as it were, war without war.[32] Those brackets were ruptured by the Treaty of Versailles, the Russian Revolution, the emergence of air power, and numberless other political and technical developments. Ever since the Great War (to emphasize one genealogy over others, for this story can be told in several ways), the concept of war has been at once absolutized (as the World Wars; as Leninist, Nazi, Maoist, and capitalist-anticommunist total war; as the unthinkable, unwinnable prospect of nuclear war) and hollowed out and fragmented (as an ever-increasing log of undeclared wars, partisan, anticolonial, and civil wars, "conflicts," acts of pacification and "peacekeeping," local actions of liberation or conquest, "ethnic cleansing"). The development of a permanent war economy in the early twentieth century began palpably to saturate the texture of civil life in the era of the Cold War, when the notion of absolute or total war was married to that of unconventional, undeclared war: under the shadow of the nuclear umbrella, not just U.S. economic might but "American culture" itself was now to be a weapon of war against an equally mobilized enemy. The health and upkeep of populations, the innumerable mechanisms of what Foucault calls governmentality or biopower—everything, in principle, could be and would be weaponized. All-pervasive though this conflict might be, however, it was also representable as figurative, as falling short of true, literal war, which could now only be nuclear. Contrary, however, to Paul Virilio's assertion that "war today is either nuclear war or nothing," the point is rather that war today is neither quite itself nor anything else, even as it is constantly being

invoked, deferred, denied, inflicted.[33] War is always-already everywhere, both as apocalyptic threat and as the quotidian reality of conflicts, ethnic cleansings, genocides, etc.; yet war defers (as nuclear
holocaust) the totality of its arrival. Postmodern theories of war often
seek to translate this paradox of war into the idiom of technocratic
strategizing: the authors of an early-twenty-first-century RAND
document *Networks and Netwars* (2001), for instance, define "netwar"
as "conflict at the less military, low-intensity, more social end of the
spectrum. . . . We had in mind actors as diverse as transnational
terrorists, criminals, and even radical activists."[34] Serving multiple
ends and devoid of clear points of origin or termination, netwar, in
such writings, can at times come across as a militaristic appropriation
of Deleuze and Guattari—which should not be surprising: sovereign
power, as we have seen, has no choice but to feed on ambiguity and
quite often does so with devastating success. The "war on terror"
offers itself as a certain culmination of this trend.[35]

But it has already become clear that the inflationary spiral of war
as a "literal" notion or praxis is inseparable from a "rhetorical" spiral.
The last century witnessed a proliferation of versions of the "war
on" formula in Anglo-American culture (a formula that, signifi-
cantly, seems to have originated in epidemiological contexts, as a
"war on typhus"). In recent decades, even literary criticism's small
swatch of the discursive universe has known theory wars and culture
wars, while the broader public sphere has endured a massively damaging war on drugs and various less consequential "wars" targeting
perceived social or moral ills. Though inseparable from the Cold
War and related developments as discussed above, these martial
tropes (all of which function differently in different contexts and
have widely varying institutional motives and resonances) are ultimately assimilable to a hypertrophied, internally dissonant figure of
war that seems part of the texture of Western modernity. Beginning,
let us say provisionally, with Hobbes and the grounding of political
life itself in an originary *bellum omnium contra omnes*, war has been
pressed into service as a trope for—or realization or extension of—
consciousness as history (Hegel, Kojève), politics (Clausewitz), class
relations (Marx), natural history (Darwin), language and cognition
(Nietzsche), and the psyche (Freud). In modernity more than ever

before, it seems, *polemos pater panton* (Heracleitus): war, the father of all things, is at the origin and at the limit, infecting and underwriting the seeming peace of the everyday. If the twentieth-century absolutization of war literalized Kant's admonition that until we successfully perform an oath of perpetual peace we remain either at war or suspended within war's potentiality, the abbreviated roll call of famous names given above suggests another way of understanding why it has become harder and harder to tell what war is (or, therefore, what "peace" is) and whether we would know it if we saw it (a predicament George Orwell allowed his newspeaking totalitarian state to parody with its lead-off epigram, "War is peace, peace is war").[36] Might there be a war so cold, a *guerre* so *drôle*, as to be invisible not just to the general public (as Bush suggested portions of the "war on terror" might be) but even to the wagers of war itself? Why not, if "war" has come to name a state constitutive of historical, political, biological, sexual, psychic, or class identity, a condition deeper and older than consciousness? Where would such a war begin or end, and how would one know?

War had thus become, by the early twentieth century, and for reasons having everything to do, of course, with the socio-material and technical developments that were transforming warfare, a profligate figure for the human condition: an ambiguous trope that, under pressure, becomes a figure of its own figurativeness, its own uncertain legibility. Like certain other ideologically and semantically charged tropes, that of "war" vacillates between a hyper-affirmation and a deconstruction of its own referential force. On the one hand (like "the body"), war functions rhetorically as the promise of a referential plenitude (or emptiness) beyond representation: it is hell, brute reality, the experience you can't know unless you've been there; in a celebratory register it becomes sublimity, the generatrix of heroism and matrix of glory.[37] On the other hand (again like "the body"), it crumbles in the grasp and reappears elsewhere.[38] War is that which transforms the uncertain into the certain and back again. On the one hand, as Samuel Weber puts it, war's "function is to institutionalize the other as enemy and thus to hold death at bay"; death thereby becomes "a state that can be inflicted upon another, upon the enemy, the result of intentional, strategic planning, a means of establishing

control and acquiring power."[39] On the other hand, from antiquity
to the present day, war has been represented as an intensified encounter with the chance (*tuchē*) that weighs on all life.[40] War generates
binary oppositions and promises the security and thrill of communal
identification and linear narrative, yet in its fog and friction the best-
laid plans go awry. (The English and French words "war" and *guerre*
both return etymologically to Old High German *werra*, "confusion."[41]) Like the sovereignty it enacts, war is both inside and outside
the law. If the notion of the "law of war" is in a sense a contradiction,
so is that of an utterly lawless war, for the notion of war has always
implied something more structured than sheer violence (it is an *"organized, legitimized,* lethal conflict," to recall the definition I gave
earlier). Schmitt offers, as so often, an incisive formulation: "To war
on both sides belongs a certain chance, a minimum of possibility for
victory. Once that ceases to be the case, the opponent becomes nothing more than an object of violent measures."[42] Yet also inherent to
war is the possibility that it will break these minimal tethers, lose all
measure, and become sheer "violent measures." In his interesting
study *The War Machine*, Daniel Pick provides these paradoxes with
a historical nuance, locating the emergence of a "powerful new vision" of war as a "driverless train" in the era of the American Civil
War and the Franco-Prussian War: a vision, that is, of war as both a
"remorselessly efficient machine" and a "deranged vehicle."[43] As a
double figure of techno-rationalization and irrationalism, he suggests, war becomes a figure for modernity's self-contradictions. Yet
that figure always turns out to be a figure of its own potential illegi-
bility, and Pick goes on to suggest that modern writing about war
discovers in its object a force that blurs and complicates that object's
representation in discourse: "the pen," he summarizes via a reading
of Clausewitz, becomes "disturbingly caught up in the 'friction' it
describes."[44] Jacqueline Rose, writing mainly about Freud but also
about Clausewitz and other writers, makes a similar point: "War . . .
operates in Freud's discourse, and not only in that of Freud, as a
limit to the possibility of absolute or total knowledge, at the same
time as such absolute or total knowledge seems over and again to be
offered as one cause—if not *the* cause—of war."[45] The death drive
explains war, but the death drive is "the speculative vanishing point

of psychoanalytic theory" (18); thus, Rose concludes, "The attempt to theorize or master war, to subordinate it to absolute knowledge, becomes a way of perpetuating or repeating war itself" (24). The fog of war thus, at the limit, names a disturbance in the rhetorical texture of war.[46]

This unruly figurativeness of war—a figurativeness thoroughly implicated in literal violence—generates uncertain crossings between war and "theory." Let me close this brief survey of the career of the figure of war with a glance at Foucault's 1976 seminar at the Collège de France, which was dedicated in part to the question: "Can war really provide a valid analysis of power relations, and can it act as a matrix for techniques of domination?"[47] Foucault unearths a tradition beginning not with Hobbes (whose figure of general warfare Foucault relegates to sheerly "figurative" or "theoretical" status) but with seventeenth-century writers of various political persuasion (from Levellers to aristocratic opponents of royal absolutism), who all understand war as "a permanent social relationship, the ineradicable basis of all relations and institutions of power" (49). Foucault feels a certain sympathy with this tradition, yet remains cautious, unwilling to reduce processes of domination to war: "Is the relation between forces in the order of politics a warlike one? I don't personally feel prepared to answer this with a definite yes or no."[48] War, here, names a moment where the theorist pauses, uncertain. A hiccup within its own theoretical explication, war is the *technē*, the cunning and the blindness, the divinity and finitude of all sovereignty, including that of theoretical understanding.

3. TERROR

What, we must now ask, is terror? And what might be made of the glide from "terrorism" to "terror" in Bush administration pronouncements and in the Western media generally? Noting what he claims to be the administration's tendency to favor the former term in 2001–2 and the latter in 2003–4, Geoffrey Nunberg observes that, while both words are vague and politically manipulable, "terror is still more amorphous and elastic" than terrorism, evoking "both the actions of terrorists and the fear they are trying to engender."[49] Furthermore, "unlike 'terrorism,' 'terror' can be applied to states as well as insurgent groups"—obviously a fact of some interest to an aggressive sovereign state eager to confront other states. And (particularly as the object of the abstractly oriented phrase "war on," rather than "war against"), terror can be represented as a disease like typhus, an "endemic condition that [can] be mitigated but not eradicated," the object of "a campaign aimed not at human adversaries but at a pervasive social plague." In the idiom of Foucault or Agamben, the war on terror can thus become a dimension of biopolitics: via terror, the terrorist becomes bare life—a germ or parasite endlessly to be exterminated. Finally, "at its most abstract, terror comes to seem as persistent and inexplicable as evil itself." Or, one could hypothesize, death itself: death is the sublime "king of terrors," per Edmund Burke's personification, because it cannot be calculated or known in advance.[50] In this sense, as Burke well understood, death is a name for an inadequacy at the heart of representation and knowledge: it is an idea "not presentable but by language" (175), vividly present only when "all is dark, uncertain, confused, terrible, and sublime to the last degree" (59). We may expect that, like war, terror will turn out to have a curiously intimate relationship with aesthetics, literature, and theory.

And indeed, like our modern notions of aesthetics, literature, democracy, human rights, revolution, and so much else in American and Western European political and cultural life, our specifically political use of the words "terror" and "terrorism" emerged at the end of the eighteenth century, forming part of the broad historical phenomenon that literary scholars call romanticism. The capitalized nominative "Terror" has, of course, a historiographical referent: it designates more or less the period between the fall of the Girondins (June 1793) and the fall of Robespierre (July 27, 1794, or 9 Thermidor). Semantically it suggests a collective fear, conditioning the social and political order; its political space is that of *mesures d'exception*, which is to say, the suspension of the political contract in a state of emergency. (The National Convention decree of October 10, 1793, suspended the recently drafted and never to be ratified Jacobin constitution, declaring that "the provisional government of France is revolutionary [*revolutionnaire*] for the duration of the war.") According to the *Dictionnaire Robert*, the first recorded uses of the French words *terroriste* and *terroriser* date from 1794; one year later, according to the *Oxford English Dictionary*, the word "terrorist" entered the English language, in Burke's fourth "Letter on a Regicide Peace" ("Thousands of those Hell-hounds called Terrorists . . . are let loose on the people") and in the Burkean *Annual Register* ("The terrorists, as they were justly denominated, from the cruel and impolitic maxim of keeping the people in implicit subjection by a merciless severity").

We obviously no longer mean quite the same thing by "terrorist" that Burke did, and of course the historical moments of 1794 and 2001 are so massively different that attempts to spin genealogical threads between them have to proceed with care. But it is important to reflect at least briefly on the Terror and its reception—above all, its Burkean, counterrevolutionary reception, for Burke's writing has shaped popularized Anglo-American representation of the French Revolution for the last two hundred years. If the French Revolution has been so often and so powerfully reduced to the image of a guillotine, this emblematic reduction of revolution to terror perhaps speaks to a certain "hatred of democracy" woven into bourgeois culture; perhaps also to a codependency of sovereignty and anxiety of the sort we have been positing here.[51] The French and American revolutions present themselves ideologically as the first fully modern identification of statehood with the living will of a national people—of a nation in action, declaring itself, founding itself in and through this declaration—and in the case of the French Revolution, this theatrical seizure of sovereignty offered its opponents the spectacle of a new sort of *illegitimate* sovereignty, insofar as the Revolution unleashed the threat of international revolution in the form of the universal claim of human rights. Later I want to look closely at a few aspects of Burke's response to the French Revolution; for the moment, let me suggest that, when Burke speaks of the illegitimacy of the Jacobin government ("the Regicides in France are not France"), he no doubt intends to evoke an ancien régime notion of rebellion or usurpation but in fact offers an early version of the quintessentially modern notion of "rogue" sovereignty, which recent American administrations have put to rhetorical work.[52] Rogue sovereignty *is* terror, and Burke urges passionately that war be declared on it. Like rebellion, rogue sovereignty triggers absolute rather than "bracketed" war (the enemy is not a *justus hostis*, a proper enemy), but unlike rebellion, which refers back to an overarching feudal order, rogue sovereignty mirrors the legitimate sovereignty of the modern state, while threatening to reproduce itself as the international proliferation of revolution. At the moment of the modern state's emergence, that is, legitimate and illegitimate sovereignty are indistinguishable, and this indistinguishability is at once sovereignty, terror, and the need to battle the contagion of their indistinction by declaring war on terror.[53]

Part of that war involved, briefly, a struggle over the political meaning of the word "terror" itself. In his important *Discourse* of February 5 in the portentous year 1794, Robespierre laid claim to this term: "Terror is nothing other than prompt, severe, inflexible justice; it is therefore an emanation of virtue; it is less a particular principle than a consequence of the general principle of democracy, applied to the most pressing needs of the nation."[54] If for Burke "terror" means anarchy (or, more precisely, a certain an-archic *archē*), for Robespierre it signifies instantaneous and absolute justice—the terror of divine justice appropriated to the *patrie*. Burke, to be sure, won this war of words: after the fall of Robespierre the word "terror" lost favor as a description of official acts of violence, and under the Thermidorians "terrorist" became for the first time a category under which people were prosecuted. "Thenceforth," as one historian summarizes, "the 'terrorists' become the Other of the republicans" in French political debate—all the more so, of course, in the increasingly Anglophone-dominated global order.[55]

Unaffirmable within the register of sanctioned public-sphere discussion, the Robespierrean claim that "terror" is "a consequence of the general principle of democracy" may nonetheless be said to echo in the many critical analyses that, over the last half-century or so, have perceived deep correspondences between democratic and totalitarian political systems.[56] Here let me reinvoke Agamben, who in *Homo Sacer* characterizes the French Revolution as a particularly important moment in the transformation of politics into biopolitics. "Declarations of rights," he suggests, "represent the originary figure of the inscription of natural life in the juridico-political order of the nation-state." Agamben here extends and translates into his own idiom Arendt's incisive critique of the fate of *les droits de l'homme* in modernity in *The Origins of Totalitarianism*. The French Revolution declared human rights to be natural (and thus unconditioned and universal) rights but also identified them with the constitution of the state. Since the nation-state remains—in our day as in Arendt's—the only effective guarantor of human rights, a fall into statelessness reduces individuals to bare life (to "the abstract nakedness of being human," as Arendt puts it).[57] The political globalization of the world in the twentieth century has produced millions of displaced persons, who, upon losing their civil rights, have effectively lost their human rights (and thus cease to be fully or properly human, becoming instead "nakedly" or "barely" human, and in extreme cases subhuman, the objects of extermination policies). "Only with a completely organized humanity could the loss of home and political status become identical with expulsion from humanity altogether."[58] All citizens are exposed to the possibility of becoming bare life precisely because—this is the point Agamben stresses—their rights, as citizens, are inscribed in their biological existence, an existence that also constitutes the subject's claim on the state and the state's claim on its subjects. For the sheer fact of having been being born (as human, with rights) has now become the "earthly foundation of the state's legitimacy and sovereignty."[59] This is the matrix of Agamben's broad claim about the camp being the *nomos* of the modern that we examined earlier and thus of his attempt to map, in the wake of Arendt and Foucault, a portion of the ambiguous interface between democratic and totalitarian twentieth-century political formations. Bare life—the moment of the citizen's inscription within the political order, to whose purity the detainee of the camp is reduced—is never an extrapolitical fact but is, rather, "a threshold in which law constantly passes over into fact and fact into law" such that "the two planes become indistinguishable."[60] It is life lived naked under the eye of sovereignty—or, in the idiom we are exploring here, life lived in and as terror. The "general principle of democracy" does not need to be held responsible for such misery, but in stressing the ease with which citizens, groups, and sometimes whole populations are reduced to "bare life" in the global order, Agamben draws attention to the diffuse workings of sovereign violence within the administered societies of Western oligarchic democracies.[61] As my discussion thus far has implied and as Judith Butler has argued, the late modern biopolitical order "reanimates a spectral sovereignty within the field of governmentality."[62] Indeed, at moments of crisis, an archaic desire to write sovereign power visibly on the body of the criminal emerges, as when the Bush administration rushed images of shackled, gagged, blindfolded, orange-suited Guantánamo detainees into view early on in its "war on terror." The administration's unyielding affirmation of its right to torture may also be understood thus: as a public claiming of the right to fashion and maintain a terrified body—and then, ambivalently and occasionally, to display this body: to put it *almost* in full view.

Let me drop this thread for awhile, however, postponing further direct discussion of the French Revolution and our contemporary "war on terror" until we have reflected on other and broader connotations of the word and concept "terror." The sheer fact that this word means "fear" means that the "war on terror" slogan can claim rich and multiple genealogies and echoes. One would never have done counting the narratives that discover the ground-tone of modernity in fear: fear provoked by the death of God, the shattering of the Ptolemaic universe, the scientific production of the infinite reaches that fill one with dread, the socially atomizing and deracinating forces of consumer capitalism and modern technics, the nuclear threat, and so on. Like war, fear emerges again and again in the Western tradition as the condition out of which human identity emerges and to which it endlessly returns: fear generates language (Condillac, and to some extent Rousseau), human self-recognition (Hegel, and especially Kojève), sovereignty and the political order (Hobbes: the Leviathan comes into being in order to protect its subjects from a limitless exposure to terror), and ideological interpellation (Althusser: What besides sheer terror can one imagine as the affective correlative of subjectification, at the moment of the policeman's "hey you!"?). Political, social, and psychic life are frequently characterized in critical narrative—the present one, to be sure, included—as sites for the production, distribution, and overall management of fear. Writing within this tradition, Brian Massumi suggests that "a history of modern nation-states could be written following the regular ebb and flow of fear rippling their surface, punctuated by outbreaks of outright hysteria."⁶³ Indeed, he asks, "what aspect of life, from the most momentous to the most trivial, has *not* become a workstation in the mass production line of fear?" (viii). That question grows all the more intriguing if one adds to it the question of whether or not one is always capable of knowing whether or not one is afraid. It is possible to claim that one either feels pain or one does not, but fear is a more slippery phenomenon. What happens when, like Freud, one opens oneself to the possibility that one could be terrified without knowing it—that the unconscious has terrors of which consciousness knows not? How counterintuitive that sounds: surely it was bad enough to have to entertain the idea that we could be at war without knowing it; can we not at least be certain of fear—the emotion that wracks the body, freezes it, turns it pale (or, in Homer, yellow-green), invades knees and stomach and sweat glands, opens orifices, turns speech into chatter?⁶⁴ What is more real than an emotion that, as a surge of adrenaline, can literally kill us? Yet we have a standard medical term for being terrified without "knowing it": trauma. A fearful event can be all the more terrible and consequential for bypassing consciousness. And even when we "know" fear, what is it that we know? Fear, considered as an affect or emotion, is like pain in this respect: capable of unmaking our world.⁶⁵ The greater our terror, the greater the shock to identity: the mind goes blank and loses control of the body; the body loses control of itself.

Without pretending to be able to provide anything akin to a genuine phenomenology of fear, I want to pursue a moment longer the peculiar status of "terror" in the modern Anglo-Latinate lexicon of the emotions. Of its near-synonyms, terror is probably closest to panic: both suggest a modality of fear particularly apt to be a group or mass phenomenon. Reflecting on group psychology in the era of mass politics, Freud calls panic (*Panik*) the "collective fear" (*Massenangst*) that accompanies the disintegration of a group when its leader, its common ego ideal, is shattered. Panic not only demonstrates the contagiousness of emotion in a group setting (with no necessary link to an objective cause, "a gigantic and senseless fear is set free"), but also what one might call emotion's impersonality: since "panic fear presupposes a relaxation in the libidinal structure of the group," it is in essence a communal or structural phenomenon, however sharply felt by individuals.[66] "Terror" differs slightly from "panic": though the latter seems more strongly associated with group experiences, the former seems, if anything, more fundamentally open to political space (one can speak of a "reign of terror" but not really of a "reign of panic"); and, as a political condition, terror resists being reduced to an individual's emotional state far more obviously than panic. A "reign of terror," of course, does not mean that everyone is emotionally terrified all the time—far from it. Here the word "terror" (and this was, once again, the decisive contribution of 1794, as we have seen), while still signifying an extreme emotional state into which the victims of political violence will at times be plunged, also conveys a whole range of emotions (anxiety, various shades of fear, even the smugness of the citizens, policemen, or state officials who imagine themselves safe) to the point that one comes to think of terror less as an emotion than as a climate or mood. Can terror be a mood in Heidegger's sense—an attunement (*Stimmung*), which is to say, "the way of our being there with one another"?[67] Is it possible to speculate that terror is the attunement proper to what Agamben calls bare life? Perhaps, though whether, in the extreme spaces of terror, one can still speak of attunement, of being-proper-to, or even of being-with in Heidegger's sense is not to be taken for granted.[68]

We may approach the same point from a slightly different vantage by noting how differently the notions of "terror" and "anxiety" shoulder metaphysical baggage. Anxiety, particularly as "the dizziness of freedom" in Kierkegaard and the early Heidegger, has proved imaginable as intrinsically human, whereas terror, fear, and fright are among the few emotions—perhaps in the end the only emotions—that, in the metaphysical tradition, humans and animals are supposed to share.[69] Yet if "fear" is taken, either in a functionalist or a Heideggerian spirit, as a response to a defined stimulus or object (and thus as the opposite of "anxiety"), then "terror" is arguably not quite that either: when I am terrified I freeze in the headlights; my sense of self shatters; my self-preservative instincts misfire; what threatens me is neither graspable as an object per se nor generalizable as the approach of nothingness, death, or freedom. We may risk the following proposal: terror is the phenomenological precondition of trauma. Terror names the possibility of *experiencing the missing of experience*. Terror does not necessarily lead to trauma in the medical sense, but the latter could not exist without the former.[70]

It is therefore possible to call on terror to name the experience—or nonexperience—of what post-Heideggerian thought calls an event. Derrida writes of the terror inherent in the idea of the "event in general": "who has ever been sure that the expectation of the Messiah is not from the start, by destination and invincibly, a fear, an unbearable terror—hence the hatred of what is awaited? And whose coming one would wish both to quicken, and infinitely to retard, as the end of the future?"[71] Fear, according to Aristotle, "may be defined as a pain or disturbance due to imagining some destructive or painful evil in the future" (*Rhetoric* II, 5: 1382a, 21–22); terror belongs to the event precisely to the extent that the event *per se* has never quite arrived and thus can never be mastered or done away with. As we saw Derrida arguing in the previous chapter, the September 11 attacks inspired terror not just because they were horrific in themselves but because they underscored the possibility of another and worse catastrophe: "Traumatism is produced by the *future*, by the *to come*, by the threat of the worst *to come*, rather than by an aggression that is 'over and done with.'"[72] In its farthest-flung phantasmatic reaches, the "war on terror" names a frantic desire to curtail the exposure to futurity that makes us the mortal beings we are.

4. TERROR IN LETTERS

Terror, the ruin of language and consciousness, can nonetheless be thought in relation to linguistic force. Primo Levi, writing of the agony that even sleeping became in Auschwitz, tells us that "one wakes up at every moment, frozen with terror, shaking in every limb, under the impression of an order shouted out by a voice full of anger in a language not understood."[73] Like so many of Levi's generalizations and descriptions, this one powerfully reminds us that the violence suffered by the camp inmate is utterly unnatural. Agamben's trope "bare life" is evocative precisely because it is neither a tautology nor an intensifier plus a noun: bare life is not *simply* life (whatever life might be). To dehumanize is not to return human beings to a hypothetical state of nature, but rather to reduce them to something far worse: "the abstract nakedness of being nothing but human."[74] The terrorized subject is interpellated as bare life through a bare speech act, a performative nearly stripped of meaning, understandable only as an order that must but cannot be understood. In Levi's account the attempt to bear witness to such terror constitutes part of the impossible but necessary task of giving testimony about Auschwitz (only the dead, Levi insists, could give uncompromised testimony), but it is what the survivor must attempt, using infinitely inadequate words.

It is easy enough to accept the idea that literature might have to struggle to remain adequate to catastrophic experience. If "the ideal of truth," as W. G. Sebald asserts, "proves itself the only legitimate reason for continuing to produce literature in the face of total destruction," the path to "unpretentious objectivity" turns out to be excruciatingly difficult.[75] Stories of catastrophic terror exceed "anyone's capacity to grasp them" (23), not just because memory fails ("the accounts of those who escaped with nothing but their lives do generally have something discontinuous about them, a curiously erratic quality so much at variance with authentic recollection that it easily suggests rumor-mongering and invention"; 24), but because the story being remembered resists being put "into any framework of reality, so that one feels some doubt of its authenticity" (88). Language itself has ghastly powers of normalization that interfere with and threaten to vitiate testimony: "The apparently unimpaired ability—shown in most of the eyewitness reports—of everyday language to go on functioning as usual raises doubt of the authenticity of the experiences they record" (25). Language's power to falsify and banalize is one of Sebald's major themes, as is his affirmation of testimony as a *literary* task. To "reveal the truth through literary efforts" (146) is to "quest for a form of language in which experiences paralyzing the power of articulation could be expressed" (150). Sebald's unsparing attention to problems of language and form offers us the insight that, pushed to the limit of its possibility, "literature" becomes the most adequate word in postromantic Western culture for the effort to speak truly of terror.

In this context it is of interest to examine a brace of texts from the mid 1940s that make broad and nonobvious claims about the link between literature and terror, and do so from a seemingly quite different vantage from that of Sebald. For Jean Paulhan, in his extraordinary and in Anglo-American contexts somewhat forgotten little book *Les fleurs de Tarbes* (1941), literature involves not so much the witnessing as the *imagining* of terror, and involves not so much a complicity with terror's victims as with the Robespierrean (or Sadean) sovereign power that seeks to discover in terror the expression of its absolute freedom. (We are now circling back once more to the French Revolution.) "One calls Terrors," Paulhan writes, "those passages in the history of nations . . . where it seems suddenly that what is needed for State governance is not cunning and method, nor even science and technics . . . but rather an extreme purity of soul, and the freshness of a communal innocence."[76] Using the Terror of 1793–94 as the figurative hinge between classicism and romanticism, Paulhan suggests that romantic, which is to say modern, literature desires to extirpate conventional linguistic forms—the commonplace, the clichéd, the rule-bound, in short, all the flowers of rhetoric. Modern literature may thus be termed a literature of terror, dreaming of an original, immediate, unmediated expressiveness, a meaning that is being. The key names in Paulhan's account are those of the French romantic and postromantic moment (Hugo to Verlaine to Rimbaud, to the surrealists of Paulhan's own time), and the overarching claim is that modern literature's desire to escape language results in an obsession with language. The more literature tries to reject rhetorical convention, the more its transparency turns refracting and refractory.

Maurice Blanchot, reviewing *Les fleurs de Tarbes* in 1941, radicalized Paulhan's study into a vibrantly paradoxical definition of literature: terror *is* literature, "or at least its soul," and this soul is condemned endlessly to lose itself in language.[77] This Paulhanian theme returns in Blanchot's great essay of 1949 "Literature and the Right to Death" as the needle with which Blanchot lets the air out of Kojèvian Hegelianism.[78] Literature, Blanchot suggests, is the one place where Hegelian negation seems to work perfectly: a writer becomes a writer by writing, acting such that a nothingness becomes something and a possibility becomes presence: "If we see work as the force of history, the force that transforms man while it transforms the world, then a writer's activity must be recognized as the highest form of work."[79] But this perfect model of work crumbles into a haunting sort of unwork or nonwork. The writer's act of negation is global and immediate; he (I shall replicate Blanchot's masculine pronoun) is free to imagine anything, no matter how fantastic—like Hegel or Kojève, for instance, he can imagine a world in which slaves become masters—and that is precisely the problem: "Insofar as he immediately gives himself the freedom he does not have, he is neglecting the actual conditions for his emancipation" (315). Global and immediate, the writer's sovereign negation negates nothing, because it offers everything instantly. We thus begin to enter the uncanny, action-ruining space of what Blanchot calls the imaginary, and at the same time we begin to register a political desire at literature's heart: a fascination with revolution. Contemplating revolution, the writer, Blanchot writes, "knows he has not stepped out of history, but history is now the void, the void in the process of realization; it is absolute freedom which has become an event. Such periods are given the name Revolution" (318). At such "fabulous moments" everything seems possible, immediately: "in them, fable speaks; in them, the speech of fable becomes action" (318). And now the title of Blanchot's essay—that intriguing transformation of man and his rights: literature and the *right* to death—begins to explain itself: in its terrible demand for transparency and purity, revolutionary action demands freedom or death, requiring the abolition of the individual's secret particularity:

> This is the meaning of the Reign of Terror. Every citizen has a right to death, so to speak. . . . When the blade falls on Saint-Just and Robespierre, in a sense it executes no one. Robespierre's virtue, Saint-Just's relentlessness, are simply their existences already suppressed, the anticipated presence of their deaths, the decision to allow freedom to assert itself completely in them and through its universality to negate the particular reality of their lives. . . . The Terrorists are those who desire absolute freedom and are fully conscious that this constitutes a desire for their own death. (319–20)

According to this account, to the extent that figures like Robespierre and Saint-Just personify Terror, they are figures of a self-annihilating purity, a death empty of significance and subjective depth.[80] The writer, Blanchot says, sees himself in the Revolution, which "attracts him because it is the time during which literature becomes history" (321). Yet literature also endlessly ruins and renders spectral the transparency and immediacy of terror. A "blind vigilance which in its attempt to escape from itself plunges deeper and deeper into its own obsession," literature "is the only rendering of the obsession of existence" (332). The obsession of existence is, for literature, that of language: "Literature is language turning into ambiguity" (341).

If one recognizes in a writer like Sebald a testimonial imperative that is also, in Paulhan or Blanchot's provocative terms, a (modern, postromantic) literary dream of terror as linguistic transparency ("the ideal of truth"), one also recognizes that Sebald's affirmation of literature's ethical task paradoxically translates into endless, scrupulous patience with linguistic deviance and mediation. That double imperative not only rules the literature of testimony but, as Sebald and Blanchot suggest in their different ways, any text we call literary—including, as we saw Miller suggesting earlier, speech acts and speech act theory, when the act or the theory begins to register within itself the disconcerting uncertainty and singularity of its own performance and terms of expression. The adjective "literary," taken in this sense, is no longer an unambiguous honorific. If I have risked calling the pseudo-sovereign declaration of war on terror a "literary" speech act, this is not to credit sovereign power with any particular sophistication, though it *is* to suggest both the cunning with which sovereignty exploits its own ambiguity and the finitude conditioning that exploitation. The Paulhan-Blanchot line of speculation has the advantage of compelling us to recognize that sovereignty, with its terror and its war on terror, is not something that literature or critical thought simply oppose from a purely external position. If one accepts the notion that the space of sovereign exception, with all its literally unspeakable horrors, cannot be firmly or absolutely distinguished from the revolutionary moment in which, as Blanchot puts it, "literature becomes history" because everything seems possible, one has affirmed a certain mutual contamination among sovereign, revolutionary, and imaginative force; one has also affirmed, as a literary task, the endless marking of the difference between sovereign power and the revolutionary moment, which is, as Blanchot says, a *fabulous* moment: it is the excess haunting sovereignty, the terror against which it wages war.

The modern literary project as Paulhan describes it—the anguished vacillation between a desire for an unmediated vision and a consciousness of linguistic mediation—is, I have argued elsewhere, a particularly concentrated version of the discourse of modern aesthetics and opens up the kind of reflection on figurative language that, in the last decades of the twentieth century, the Anglo-American academy began to call "theory." And "theory" is, in fact, another word that, since the era of the French Revolution, has been associated with terror. "Theory" and "theorist" and various cognates ("speculative," "speculation") rank among Burke's favored pejoratives in the *Reflections* and in his other counterrevolutionary texts. William Wordsworth's thirty-line apostrophe to Burke in the 1850 *Prelude* grants appropriately explosive metrical emphasis to Burke's accomplishment as he

> Declares the vital power of social ties
> Endeared by Custom; and with high disdain,
> Exploding upstart Theory, insists
> Upon the allegiance to which men are born.[81]

"Theory," in Wordsworth's or Burke's usage, tends to mean abstractly rational, systematic thought, yet Burke's strictures about theory also tend to grant it an uncanny, spectral, excessive agency. It is precisely because the French Revolution "is a Revolution of doctrine and theoretick dogma" that it is sublimely uncontainable and threatens to spread across Europe, or indeed around the world, like disease, money, and newsprint.[82] David Simpson has argued that one can trace late-twentieth-century animadversions about theory in Britain and, mutatis mutandis, the United States back to these eighteenth- and early-nineteenth-century roots, as though denunciations of systematic thinking even today were still haunted by the "ghost of Robespierre, the coldest of the ruthless abstractionists."[83] His remarks help contextualize the frigid inhumanity that antitheoretical writers so frequently ascribe to theory's totemic figure in the American academy, Paul de Man: a critic whose work focuses with exemplary intensity on the ways in which the problematic of reading aligns with that of terror. Reading, for de Man, originates in and returns endlessly to fear—but the whole "theoretical" point is that "fear," at least in this context, is the opacity of a text that must and yet cannot be read with certainty. I cannot do more than gesture here toward a topic that elsewhere I have tried to examine in some detail; perhaps it will suffice to recall that the allegory of reading that de Man extracts from various texts by Rousseau takes off from a counterintuitive interpretation of Rousseau's parable, in the *Essay on the Origin of Language*, of the primitive man who, meeting other men for the first time, feels afraid and names them "giants," thereby transforming a hypothesis (the men might be dangerous) into a certainty. "The metaphor is blind, not because it distorts objective data, but because it presents as certain what is, in fact, a mere possibility. . . . By calling [the other man] a 'giant,' one freezes hypothesis, or fiction, into fact and makes fear, itself a figural state of suspended meaning, into a definite, proper meaning devoid of alternatives."[84] Fear—at least "in theory"—comes into being as the ongoing, and always imperfect, obliteration of its own constitutive uncertainty.[85]

As the theory of fear (as uncertainty), theory becomes fearful, turning away from and resisting itself and inspiring fear in those who, seeking to put uncertainty (as fear) aside, condemn theory as an excess of enlightened rationality turned obscurantism. The word "obscurantism" is not intended as mine here, but as John Searle's. Here is a quote from Searle's negative review of Jonathan Culler's *On Deconstruction* in *The New York Review of Books* in 1983, back when the scandal of theory was still relatively fresh: "Michel Foucault once characterized Derrida's prose style to me as *obscurantisme terroriste*. The text is written so obscurely that you can't figure out exactly what the thesis is (hence *obscurantisme*) and then when one criticizes it, the author says, *Vous m'avez mal compris; vous êtes idiot* (hence *terroriste*)."[86] I would suggest that the adjective *terroriste*—we are speaking "French" here—is organizing this little namedropping anecdote because two centuries' worth of associations, filiations, and figurative transports have woven a context in which obscurity, terror, and reason—here figured as a kind of ruthless ruse, the reader-trap of *Vous m'avez mal compris; vous êtes idiot*—conjoin to condition the reception of something called "theory." We may seem rather far from romanticism, reading Searle on Derrida. But if one thinks about Burke's early interest in the link between obscurity and terror in the *Enquiry*, about what he says in that treatise about the arbitrariness and power of words, and about the ability of language to achieve sublimity by surpassing its own representational function; if one considers all the ways that "French" as the foreign, but perhaps not quite foreign enough, language of theory has played a role in the theory wars—Searle expects you to be able to understand these snippets of French: monolingual middlebrow American reader of *The New York Review of Books* though you be, you'd better understand these bits of symbolic obscurity, otherwise *vous êtes idiot*; French, in other words, has always already crossed the Channel and hopped over the Atlantic, even though it needs to be marked off as foreign and expelled—if one keeps all this in mind, the era of Burke and Wordsworth, Rousseau and Robespierre may not seem so very distant after all.

5. ROMANTICISM AND THE WAR ON TERROR

Since I have been proposing a line of argument that, via numerous mediations, refers the war on terror back to the French Revolution and the opening of the era of human rights, mass politics, and biopolitical power, let me pause now and ask that we take a closer look at certain aspects of Burke's counterrevolutionary writing. From the start—from Wollstonecraft and Hazlitt through Arnold and down to our own time—there has been a tradition of reading Burke as both the fount or father of modern conservatism and as a self-divided figure, covertly akin to and in sympathy with the revolutionary Jacobin he opposes.[87] Close readings of the *Reflections* reveal a Burke repeating what he condemns and worrying the status of borders and distinctions that he not only cannot police but also cannot help systematically violating. Writing in the great political philosophical tradition that descends from Aristotle through Hobbes, Locke, and Rousseau, Burke, after numerous rhetorical twists and turns, produces a social-contract justification of governmental authority ("society is indeed a contract"[88]). If he rejects the declaration of the rights of men and the declaration of the Republic, he does not reject declaration. A sovereign speech act opens the space of sovereign right and of social and political being, though the locus of its power is ambiguous. At times Burke refers the social contract back to a divine fiat, an "oath," presumably sworn by God to himself, that holds together the universe: "Society is indeed a contract. . . . Each contract of each particular state is but a clause in the great primeval contract of eternal society linking the lower with the higher natures, connecting the visible and the invisible world, according to a fixed compact sanctioned by the inviolable oath which holds all physical and all moral natures, each in their appointed place."[89] At other times Burke, whose references to traditional religious faith never come across as very deeply felt, offers a more secular account of society's origins.[90] In both cases one notes creeping complications. If the divine "inviolable oath" seems to subordinate the universe and its deity to a strange, superdivine linguistic power, the secular (and equally inviolable) oath emerges out of paradox and fictionality, for the fundamental claim of Burkean conservatism is that we never gets to the end or the bottom of the contract, which always precedes us. The "People" does not and has never existed in a state of nature: "it is wholly artificial, and made like other legal fictions by common agreement."[91] (Put in more lapidary—even Wildean—fashion: "Art is man's nature."[92]) The "legal fiction" of the people has been made by "common agreement"—by a people that is not yet a people but must be a people in order to decree itself a people. Like the divine oath, the secular one implies an endless sequence of authorities by whom and to whom the oath is sworn. At the origin is a nonorigin, a "fiction"—in the terms we have elaborated, a *literary* speech act.

Fictionality, however, is aestheticized through temporal mediation. Man's "art" becomes "nature" by way of a temporality borrowed from the natural order:

Our political system is placed in a just correspondence and symmetry with the order of the world, and with the mode of existence decreed to a permanent body composed of transitory parts; wherein, by the disposition of a stupendous wisdom, moulding together the great mysterious incorporation of the human race, the whole, at one time, is never old, or middle-aged, or young, but in a condition of unchangeable constancy, moves on through the varied tenor of perpetual decay, fall, renovation, and progression. Thus, by preserving the method of nature in the conduct of the state, in what we improve we are never wholly new; in what we retain we are never wholly obsolete. By adhering in this manner and on these principles to our forefathers, we are guided not by the superstition of antiquarians, but by the spirit of philosophic analogy. In this choice of inheritance we have given to the frame of our polity the image of a relation in blood; binding up the constitution of our country with our dearest domestic ties; adopting our fundamental laws into the bosom of our family affections; keeping inseparable, and cherishing with the warmth of all their combined and mutually reflected charities, our state, our hearths, our sepulchres, and our altars.[93]

This famous passage retains traces of the instability of the originary speech act, both in the self-conscious fictionality and literariness of its terms ("philosophic analogy"; an "image of a relation in blood") and, perhaps more tellingly, in the strange figure of an impossible, contradictory choice: "In this *choice of inheritance* we have given to the frame of our polity the image of a relation in blood." The oxymoronic figure of choice recurs in Burke's subsequent paragraph, in which "we" are said to choose nature and the breast itself: "All your sophisters cannot produce anything better adapted to preserve a rational and manly freedom than the course that we have pursued, who have *chosen our nature* rather than our speculations, *our breasts* rather than our inventions" (121, my emphasis). Inheritance, nature, and the breast are, of course, three things that one by definition cannot choose; indeed, the rhetorical function of the figures of inheritance and nature in Burke's polemic is precisely that of marking a fatality and a necessity. It is as an "*entailed* inheritance" that the polity is forbidden to vote itself out of existence and embark on revolution (119, Burke's emphasis). Burke's strained, radically fictional figure of choice relays the volatility of the original Austinian speech act upon which modern sovereignty rests.

The haunting trope of impossible, excessive choice culminates in a passage in which Burke admits into his text, however reluctantly, a revolutionary moment in which a "necessity that is not chosen but chooses" justifies "a resort to anarchy":

> It is the first and supreme necessity only, a necessity that is not chosen but chooses, a necessity paramount to deliberation, that admits no discussion, and demands no evidence, which alone can justify a resort to anarchy. This necessity is no exception to the rule; because this necessity itself is a part too of that moral and physical disposition of things to which man must be obedient by consent or force; but if that which is only submission to necessity should be made the object of choice, the law is broken, nature is disobeyed, and the rebellious are outlawed, cast forth, and exiled, from this world of reason, and order, and peace, and virtue, and fruitful penitence, into the antagonist world of madness, discord, vice, confusion, and unavailing sorrow. (195)

Unlike Hobbes, who with brutal pragmatism equates the Leviathan's failure to protect his subjects with the loss of his right to rule, Burke never specifies what sort of event would be required to strip a sovereign of sovereignty—what such a "first and supreme necessity" justifying "a resort to anarchy" would look like. His insistence that "this necessity is no exception to the rule" holds only to the degree that the rule, as always in the space of sovereign exception, has become indistinguishable from its suspension at the moment of sovereign decision or choice. How can one know whether one is choosing or whether necessity has chosen? Whether one has "submitted to necessity" or whether one has exceeded law, reason, and order in the moment of choice—a choice so excessive as to be that of "inheritance" or "nature" itself?

The terrifying, excessive moment of choice is always, in the Burkean text, a choice of war: a war on terror, by way of terror. In Burke's writings after 1790, this theme becomes prominent, above all in the *Letters on a Regicide Peace* of 1795–97, which insists that the war on terror must be a total war, fought without remission or mercy:

> We are at war with a system, which, by its essence, is inimical to all other Governments, and which makes peace or war, as peace

and war may best contribute to their subversion. It is with an armed doctrine that we are at war. It has, by its essence, a faction of opinion, and of interest, and of enthusiasm, in every country. To us it is a Colossus which bestrides our channel. It has one foot on a foreign shore, the other upon the British soil. (*Regicide Peace* I, 19)

The sheer existence of the Jacobins constitutes an act of war that requires war of us. The war is a civil war, both because Europe is "virtually one great state" (*Regicide Peace* I, 80) such that laws of vicinage or neighborhood apply (*Regicide Peace* I, 82–83) and because the opponent is everywhere: on the one hand, he is the non-European, the cannibal (*Regicide Peace* I, 76–77), the Moslem, or the Jew (*Regicide Peace* II, 118, *passim*), yet, on the other hand, he is the neighbor next door. Though the Revolution is always already all-too-French-foreign, what this really means is that it has no certain origin or end. At one point Burke even suggests that the Jacobin disease originated in England: "I have reason to be persuaded, that it was in this Country, and from English Writers and English Caballers, that France herself was instituted in this revolutionary fury" (*Regicide Peace* IV, 307). More tellingly, in the *Reflections*, Burke savors the image of a double counterfeit and the figure of a line crossed and recrossed as he imagines French revolutionaries being inspired by Britain's own revolution and then themselves inspiring British Jacobins: "We ought not, on either side of the water, to suffer ourselves to be imposed upon by the counterfeit wares which some persons, by a double fraud, export to you in illicit bottoms, as raw commodities of British growth though wholly alien to our soil, in order afterwards to smuggle them back again into this country, manufactured after the newest Paris fashion of an improved liberty."[94] The figure of the line is Burke's master trope, on which all law and prophecy hang: "The speculative line of demarcation, where obedience ought to end, and resistance must begin, is faint, obscure, and not easily definable. It is not a single act, or a single event, which determines it."[95] And it is the inevitable blurring of the line even as it is drawn that generates terror and counterterror. Burke and Robespierre, skewed doubles, root out conspiracies that proliferate infinitely, prosecuting a war in which sovereignty and terror define each other in and through their mutual uncertainty.

6. TOWARD PERPETUAL PEACE

To sum up, hyperbolically: romanticism, giving us literature, theory, nationalism and internationalism, human rights, revolution, "rogue" sovereignty, and biopolitics, declared a war on terror that we inherit as part of modernity itself—though the inheritance is an uncertain one, for we will never be certain of this declaration's locutionary shape, illocutionary status, or perlocutionary reach. In consequence, the declaration of war on terror is at once the most obvious, overde-termined, and obscure speech act of our era. Because this declaration declares absolute (and yet virtual) war, it could only be performed plausibly—we will not say "felicitously," for it destroys the difference between felicitous and infelicitous performatives—by the executive officer of a superpower in an era of geopolitical strategizing and global telecommunication. Taken to its limit as a declaration of reli-gious war on "evil" itself—and on everything "terror" signifies in modernity—it is a profession of faith that issues in the cynical tactics of a sovereignty that understands itself to be scrabbling for its rights. This declaration is *the* exemplary modern sovereign speech act: it unleashes war as terror and terror as war, while remaining a fabu-lous, even at times risible utterance, "in a peculiar way hollow or void"—a sovereign performative that exacerbates the uncertain on-tology of sovereign power and the nagging obscurity of the declara-tion's own keywords. The declaration of war on terror may thus be taken not just as one aspect of the ever-tightening regime of modern technics but as the very motto of techno-metaphysical domination. What other phrase better captures, on the one hand, what Heidegger calls the modern techno-project of regulating and securing (*Steue-rung und Sicherung*)—the imperative to objectify and put on order, stockpile and secure—and, on the other hand, that project's disloca-tion of place, time, and identity?[96]

But though I am stressing its multilayered exemplarity, I am not seeking to characterize the declaration and discourse of "war on ter-ror" as ineluctable. It certainly is not ineluctably fated to remain a viable political slogan. The weakening of U.S. hegemony in coming decades will surely produce new global dispositions and phantasms of sovereign power. Those future cultural, socioeconomic, and military contexts may well prove even more bellicose and terrible than the present ones, but the particular Western, and particularly Anglo-American idiom of war on terror as we have traced it here will not necessarily survive except in the memory of historians. Even in the short term, and within a domestic American compass, one can imagine the bitter lexicon of the Bush administration falling into disrepute and desuetude, at least so long as the nation is spared another major terrorist strike. The war on terror, like everything else, is forgettable. And it is not any less so for having marshaled the language of the absolute, and in terms that lay claim so powerfully to a sprawling Western, Christian, and modern tradition.

In such a context, what would it mean to affirm that peace has a chance? If war has become a concept as obscure as its reality is terrible, the idea of peace cannot hope to be easy of access. "Peace," like the French *paix*, derives from the Latin *pax, pacis*, which in turn comes from Indo-European words meaning "fasten" or "fetter." In this linguistic cluster, peace is a pact (*pactum*); it is a contract, an act of binding, emerging out of a world of bargaining, payment, and promising. The German word *Friede* has a different genealogy, returning to the Indo-European **pri-*, out of which come words meaning "near" or "by." The Kluge etymological dictionary of the German language proposes that *Friede*, in its root meaning "would therefore be more or less 'being-together-with' [*Beieinandersein*] in the sense of 'reciprocal handling within the tribe.'" *Friede* comes from the same root as the German and English *Freund*, "friend" (which in its oldest versions conveys kinship), and *frei*, "free" (which in its root, **prijo-*, means that which we own and love: that which is near us, beside us, ready to hand). We may leave aside the question of what traces the Hebrew *shalom* and Greek *eirene* have left on the European-Christian tradition; of interest here is the way in which this double tradition comprised by, on the one hand, the Latinate sense of peace as a contract or promise and, on the other hand, the Germanic sense of peace as being-together rhymes with two prominent traditions of thinking about peace in the modern world. On the one hand, corresponding in some ways to the idea of peace as a true being-together, there is Abrahamic millenarianism in its various traditions and forms; on the other hand, overlapping quite strikingly with the idea of peace as a contract or promise, there is the eirenic cosmopolitanism we associate generally with the Enlightenment and particularly with the writings of the Abbé de Saint-Pierre, Rousseau, and Kant on the possibility of "perpetual peace" among nations. The chiliastic or millenarian tradition associates peace with the end of history; the cosmopolitan tradition understands peace as the suspension, through legal and social contracts, of violent political conflict.

This familiar and often useful contrast between theological and political notions of peace, however, blurs upon closer inspection. I have occasionally invoked Kant's essay "Toward Perpetual Peace" (1795) in these pages, and I want to conclude by paying homage to this famous and enduring call for peace as *pactum* in the Western tradition. As noted previously, Kant's is a text that on one point refuses all compromise: peace must be perpetual or it is not truly itself; no peace treaty establishing anything less than perpetual peace is genuinely a peace treaty. "No treaty of peace [*Friedensschluß*] that tacitly reserves issues for a future war shall be held valid. For if this were the case, it would be a mere truce, a suspension of hostilities, not peace, which means the end of all hostilities, so much so that even to modify it by 'perpetual' [or 'eternal': *ewig*] smacks of pleonasm."[97] (196/107). Such a declaration of peace, Kant tells us, forbids any holding back, any mental reservation (*reservatio mentalis*). It must be a fully intended, absolutely transparent speech act—as unmediated and instantaneous as Robespierrean justice—and under the terms of Kant's critical philosophy it would be, a priori, an impossible speech act. "Without the presupposition of time," as Kant had pithily commented in a popularizing essay published a few months earlier, "The End of All Things" (1794), "nothing can be thought of."[98] As Peter Fenves comments: "The slogan 'eternal peace' can be announced only under the sign of failure, because the term eternity does not belong either to the vocabulary of politics or to the lexicon of the 'critical enterprise.'"[99] Fenves is referring here in part to the cagy, complexly satirical reflection on the phrase *Zum ewigen Frieden* ("toward perpetual/eternal peace") with which Kant's text begins. Kant not only uses this phrase as his title but places it above his

opening sentence as an epigraph, thereby launching his essay as a
reflection on an "inscription" (*Überschrift*) that Kant declares a grim
joke and an enigma, even as he places his text under its sign:

> ## Toward Perpetual Peace
>
> Whether this satirical inscription on that Dutch innkeeper's sign
> on which a graveyard was painted, holds for human beings in gen-
> eral, or especially for heads of state who can never get enough of
> war, or perhaps only for philosophers who dream that sweet
> dream, may be set aside.

I cannot begin to summarize adequately the various complexities of
this introductory section or even of this introductory sentence, but
we may note in passing the gnomic density of this *satirische Überschrift*. On the one hand, it seems descriptive of a movement toward
a goal, but on the other hand, as Kant will make clear, it relays the
force of moral law and therefore can and must be a command or
exhortation: "To perpetual peace!" Even the preposition here, let
alone the adjective and the noun, causes problems: *zu* often means
"toward," but it can also mean "at," as in *chez* or *apud* (if you are at
home in German, you are *zu Hause*, and if you are at an inn called
Eternal Peace, you are *zum Ewigen Frieden*). We may and ought to
be on the way toward perpetual peace, but we may be and ought to
be in some way already there without knowing it, and then there is
the problem that this inn may be a grave. Thus Kant, an innkeeper
with a taste for morbid satire, extends to us his text's hospitality.

If peace is such that even to modify it by "perpetual" smacks of
pleonasm, every time we speak of peace we cannot help speaking of
what we cannot properly conceptualize. Every time we promise
peace, we make an impossible promise. The idiom of metaphysics
infects that of politics; the millenarian meaning of peace insinuates
itself into the *pactum*. Yet as "peace" becomes the site of a certain
excess within language and thought, a nonapocalyptic openness to
the future may be said to emerge. On the one hand, one could say
that perpetual peace is unlivable, and therefore must constantly
threaten to resemble its dark double, the global graveyard that Kant
several times evokes in a treatise obsessed by the possibility of failure,

apocalypse, and death. As an impossible figure, peace remains constitutively exposed to a failure it cannot accept, and in hock to images of failure by which it cannot help being entranced.[100] Yet on the other hand one could say that the impossibility of this peace leaves its mark—as the unthought thought of peace—on our daily lives.[101] Peace, for Kant, is an immediate duty; however uncognizable and impossible, it *must* be thought about and worked toward. Kant's treatise is filled with pragmatic and thoroughly concrete proposals, some specific to his time, some of relevance to the present day (abolish standing armies; prohibit national-debt financing, which makes it too easy for nations to raise and maintain armies; base the rights of nations on a federation of free states; etc.). The infinite, radically fictional or literary imperative of peace drives these thoughts and opens the text to supplementation and change. Pursuant to this reading, latter-day Kantians will labor to realize, for instance (this list is perpetually extendable): a stronger United Nations; a world criminal court; the global enforcement of human rights; the expansion of the concept of said rights to include economic rights, the right to sanctuary, sexual freedom, etc.; the eradication of torture and political prisons; the demilitarization of nations, including the most powerful; the prosecution of war criminals, including the most sovereign. Kant's text commits itself to the impossible so as to call on us to take up the pragmatic, everyday work of being cosmopolitan citizens. As David L. Clark puts it, Kant proceeds *as if* peace were possible; his treatise, miming the form of a treaty, unfolds as an act of faith, promising in the absence of guarantees and affirming its radical exposure to failure, loss, and the other—its vulnerability, in short, to the uncertainty and futurity we have here called terror.[102] Perhaps we could say that peace commands us *as if* it were an imperative, thereby opening the fragile possibility of an other peacetime, an other being-with or living-together. Eternity, Fenves suggests, may in this spirit be taken as a term designating "a time for something other than the temporal continuum," a time that "could take place at *any* time."[103] Such is the time of a promise of a living-together that would no longer be familial or tribal and a future that would no longer be apocalyptic: a peace that would no longer be a war on terror.

NOTES

1. The *Oxford English Dictionary* lists a number of rare or obsolete definitions that recall the word's Latin origin ("possessing certain physical virtues"; "morally virtuous"; "effective, potent, powerful"; "[of herbs] possessing specific virtues"). "Virtual" also has a technical meaning in optics: "the apparent focus or image resulting from the effect of reflection or refraction upon rays of light."

2. See Jacques Derrida, "Autoimmunity: Real and Symbolic Suicides: A Dialogue with Jacques Derrida," in Giovanna Borradori, *Philosophy in a Time of Terror: Dialogues with Jürgen Habermas and Jacques Derrida* (Chicago: University of Chicago Press, 2003), 85–136. I discuss this interview in my first chapter.

3. Jean Baudrillard, *The Spirit of Terrorism*, trans. Chris Turner (London: Verso, 2003), 5.

4. As when, to take a small and everyday instance, a memory we cherish as particularly vivid turns out to be the memory of a photograph. Benjamin's writing about shock is spread out over many texts, but see in particular his great essay "On Some Motifs in Baudelaire," in *Illuminations: Essays and Reflections*, trans. Harry Zohn (New York: Schocken Books, 1969), 155–200.

5. See Benedict Anderson, *Imagined Communities: Reflections on the Origin and Spread of Nationalism* (1983; New York: Verso, 1991). For my discussion of nationalism and iterability, which draws on Anderson's classic study and offers a mild critique of it, see *The Politics of Aesthetics: Nationalism, Gender, Romanticism* (Stanford: Stanford University Press, 2003), esp. 49–55.

6. Karl Marx and Friedrich Engels, *Basic Writings on Politics and Philosophy*, ed. Lewis S. Feuer (New York: Doubleday, 1959), 6.

7. Lawrence Wechsler, *A Miracle, a Universe: Settling Accounts with Torturers* (New York: Pantheon Books, 1990), 122. I was led to this quote by Avery F. Gordon, who cites Wechsler's citation and comments astutely: "What is this enemy if not a conjuring malevolent specter? It is not what it seems to the

visible eye. It has extraordinary powers to take familiar shapes and to surreptitiously mess up boundaries and proper protocols" (Avery F. Gordon, *Ghostly Matters: Haunting and the Sociological Imagination* [Minneapolis: University of Minnesota Press, 1997], 125).

8. See Slavoj Žižek, *The Sublime Object of Ideology* (London: Verso, 1989), 11–53: "the illusion is not on the side of knowledge, it is already on the side of reality itself, of what the people are doing" (32). Žižek offers a number of vividly argued examples: "When individuals use money, they know very well there is nothing magical about it. . . . So, on an everyday level, the individuals know perfectly well that there are relations between people behind the relations between things. The problem is that in their social activity itself, in what they are doing, they are acting as if money, in its material reality, is the immediate embodiment of wealth as such. They are fetishists in practice, not in theory" (31).

9. Jacques Derrida, *Specters of Marx: The State of the Debt, the Work of Mourning, and the New International*, trans. Peggy Kamuf (New York: Routledge, 1994), 136.

10. Torture often involves raw sexual abuse, but the recourse to women as torture devices has to be one of the weirder outcomes of the mix of anthropological fantasizing and Army lore that produced the heady brew of approved abusive practices for Guantánamo, Abu Ghraib, Baghram, and elsewhere. What are we to say of a "technique" called "Invasion of Space by a Female," duly noted in the official interrogation log of Detainee 063 (Mohammed al-Qahtani) as having been applied to him, along with various other torments, on Day 14, December 6, 2002? My source is Philippe Sands, *Torture Team: Rumsfeld's Memo and the Betrayal of American Values* (New York: Palgrave Macmillan, 2008), 13. According to Sands, the Fox-TV show "24" played a role in raising the erotic temperature of the brainstorming sessions on interrogation techniques led by Diane Beaver (Staff Judge Advocate at Guantánamo), who signed off on the new "techniques." Many books have now appeared documenting the high-level criminal involvement of the Bush administration in this ugly history: see, in addition to Sands, Erich Lichtblau, *Bush's Law: The Remaking of American Justice* (New York: Pantheon, 2008), and Philip Gourevitch and Errol Morris, *Standard Operating Procedure* (New York: Penguin, 2008). A growing number of films and television shows have recently focused on U.S. torture practices: among them are *The Road to Guantánamo*, dir. Michael Winterbottom (2006); *Taxi to the Dark Side*, dir. Alex Gibney (2007); *Rendition*, dir. Gavin Hood (2007); *Standard Operating Procedure*, dir. Errol Morris (2008).

11. David Simpson, *9/11: The Culture of Commemoration* (Chicago: University of Chicago Press, 2006), 142. By the time I read this brilliant and eloquent

study, most of the main body of my text had been drafted and part of it had been published as an article. Though I have incorporated some references to Simpson's text into mine, inevitably there remain a number of unflagged points of overlap where we share themes and emphases. Our styles and broader projects are sufficiently different that I hope readers familiar with one text will not be dissuaded from engaging the other.

12. The uncontrollability of haunting cannot simply be equated with the leakage of information, of course; the latter, whether calculated or not, plays an integral role in the deployment of sovereign terror. The state's power to make people disappear needs to be at least sporadically visible if populations are to be managed through fear. Yet the open secret of disappearance cannot be utterly controlled by sovereign power either, particularly in the contemporary context. A full analysis of the Bush administration's record in this area would need to take into account effects generated by the outsourcing of torture and incarceration not just to client nations but to private contractors (this being a small part of the ongoing capitalization of special-operations warfare, disaster relief, etc.).

13. Simpson, 9/11, 144.

14. Judith Butler, *Precarious Life: The Powers of Mourning and Violence* (London and New York: Verso, 2004), xii.

1. VIRTUAL TRAUMA

1. I discuss the phrase and notion of a "war on terror" in the subsequent chapter.

2. For instance: newly heroic (and politically exploitable) connotations for the idiom "let's roll"; newly grim or ghoulish ones for "boxcutter" or "Fresh Kills." I should probably gloss that last example, which falls slightly beyond the circle of generally known facts about 9/11, though it exemplifies the way in which this tragedy seems able to exert a gravitational pull on randomly generated semiotic materials. Fresh Kills Landfill, named for the Fresh Kills Estuary on the west shore of Staten Island (the name itself being a distortion from the Dutch), was from 1947 to 2001 the major dumping ground for the City of New York. Slated to be closed and transformed into wetlands in the spring of 2001, it was temporarily reopened (September 2001–July 2002) as the forensic site and processing ground for the roughly one million tons of debris removed from the World Trade Center site. A traveling exhibit (now a Web page), "Recovery," has documented the search for human remains and material evidence during this period: see http://www.nysm.nysed.gov/exhibits/long term/documents/recovery.pdf. Fresh Kills is in the news as I write this note: a lawsuit was filed in 2006 by a group representing families of 9/11 victims seeking proper burial for discoverable human remains in the former landfill.

3. Dominick LaCapra, *Representing the Holocaust: History, Theory, Trauma* (Ithaca: Cornell University Press, 1994), 220. Scholarship on historical trauma has become substantial: for a broad and theoretically sophisticated recent study, see Jenny Edkins, *Trauma and the Memory of Politics* (Cambridge: Cambridge University Press, 2003).

4. The present essay is paying homage, of course, to two great writers, Susan Sontag and Jacques Derrida, who died in the fall of 2004, but it is not intended as a memorial to them. It is motivated by a wish to think about aspects of its subject matter that the work of these writers helps illuminate. To be sure, Derrida has left a deeper mark on the present essay than Sontag: if there is a single thinker whose name deserves to be associated with the effort and imperative to read or understand a phenomenon of the order of "September 11," it is arguably Derrida. One reason why he was able to offer such richly textured reflections in his interview with Giovanna Borradori on October 22, 2001 (see note 9, below), is because he had behind him some four decades of relevant philosophical thinking (in addition to more than three decades of visible activity as a public intellectual speaking out on political and social issues). From his early studies of Husserl to his last texts, he pressured and undermined (though never simply *erased*) the difference between empirical and conceptual or ideal phenomena, as part of a sustained meditation on the "event" that took many forms, most famously that of a meditation on what Western culture has tagged as "writing."

5. Benedict Anderson, *Imagined Communities: Reflections on the Origin and Spread of Nationalism* (New York: Verso, 1983), 24 Anderson borrows the phrase "homogeneous empty time" from Walter Benjamin. I analyze Anderson's writings about nationalism in my *The Politics of Aesthetics: Nationalism, Gender, Romanticism* (Stanford: Stanford University Press, 2003), 45–73. Dates, of course, have always been chargeable with political significance (as the old song about Guy Fawkes Night emphasizes: "Remember, remember the fifth of November"), but the name-date per se, as temporal marker and toponym, seems to flourish particularly in revolutionary and republican contexts from the late eighteenth century on. The names of holidays inherited from Catholic and pre-Christian calendars (All Hallows' Eve, Christmas, El Dìa de los Muertos, saints' days, and so forth) typically include reference to some identity or event other than a sheer numerical date. A hybrid and contested ceremonial date such as May 1—which, of course, has ancient pagan foundations and now, as International Workers' Day, commemorates the workers executed in the wake of the 1886 Haymarket Riots (except in the United States, where a McCarthy-era Congress designated May 1 "Loyalty Day")—may be said to have acquired its properly "name-date" elements in the modern era of bourgeois nationalism and proletarian internationalism.

6. According to the Wikipedia entry on 9-1-1, the emergency number was in fact originally introduced as "nine-eleven," but since it was found that in panic situations people sometimes looked vainly for an "eleven" on their dials, the phrase was altered to "nine-one-one." I have not been able to verify that claim, but have been able to cross-check the following information: the number 9-1-1 was established in 1968 by ATT in response to a recommendation from the President's Commission on Law Enforcement and Administration of Justice in 1967, though only in 1999 was a Congressional bill signed designating it as the official emergency number. The number still does not cover some rural areas of the United States and Canada. For information on the history of 9-1-1, see http://www.nena9-1-1.org, and http://en.wikipedia.org/wiki/9-1-1.

7. In Europe, the telephone emergency number is 112 (in Britain it is 999), so familiarity with the American 9-1-1 code cannot simply be assumed. The date of September 11 seems to have been chosen, probably by Mohamed Atta, in mid-August 2001, when the hijackers' airline tickets began to be booked. (Khalid Sheikh Mohammed, the mastermind of the attacks, was notified of the chosen date by coded message about that time.) Atta, who had, of course, received his pilot training in the United States, may well have had the North American emergency number in mind, but all we learn from the *9/11 Commission Report* is that Atta suggested to his co-conspirator Ramzi Binalshibh that "the attacks would not happen until after the first week in September, when Congress reconvened." See *The 9/11 Commission Report: Final Report of the National Commission on Terrorist Attacks upon the United States* (New York: Norton, 2004), 248–49.

8. There are other significant September 11s in Western history, as David Simpson reminds us—at the same time reminding us that such patterns present us with a sheerly "paranoid coherence": "the assassination of Allende on September 11, 1973; the British Mandate in Palestine on September 11, 1922; the U.S. invasion of Honduras on September 11, 1919; and the defeat of the Ottoman armies before the gates of Vienna on September 11, 1683" (David Simpson, *9/11: The Culture of Commemoration* [Chicago: University of Chicago Press, 2006], 14). One could extend such paranoid reasoning: flipped into European day-month mode, "9/11" becomes November 9, the date both of the night of terror called *Kristallnacht* in Germany in 1938 and of the fall of the Berlin Wall in 1989.

9. Jacques Derrida, "Autoimmunity: Real and Symbolic Suicides," in Giovanna Borradori, *Philosophy in a Time of Terror: Dialogues with Jürgen Habermas and Jacques Derrida* (Chicago: University of Chicago Press, 2003), 88, 94.

10. Jacques Derrida, "Shibboleth," in Jacques Derrida, *Sovereignties in Question: The Poetics of Paul Celan*, ed. Thomas Dutoit and Outi Pasanen (New York: Fordham University Press, 2005), 2.

11. One is by a professional photographer and one by a police officer: see Joel Meyerowitz, *Aftermath: World Trade Center Archive* (New York: Phaidon Press, 2006); and John Botte, *Aftermath: Unseen 9/11 Photos by a New York City Cop* (New York: Regan Books, 2006). Another recent book focused on photography and 9/11 is David Friend, *Watching the World Change: The Stories Behind the Images of 9/11* (New York: Farrar, Strauss, and Giroux, 2006). The summer of 2006 also saw the appearance of *The 9/11 Report: A Graphic Adaptation*, illustrated by Sid Jacobson and Ernie Colon (New York: Hill and Wang, 2006).

12. The conspiracy-theory literature on 9/11 is staggeringly profuse. A good place to begin is with the film *Loose Change* (first version, 2005; revised versions in 2006), written and directed by Dylan Avery. Versions of this film are available for free viewing on the Internet, and there are numerous sites supporting or debunking it. Of the many books written from this perspective, one of the most influential has been Thierry Meyssan, *9/11: The Big Lie* (London: Carnot, 2002). The adaptability of 9/11 to conspiracy theory and by extension to the thriller genre (the brilliantly written *9/11 Commission Report* often delivers the page-turning pleasures of a Robert Ludlum novel) deserves further analysis. In the next chapter I shall argue that the sovereign and the terrorist become skewed doubles in late-twentieth-century and early-twenty-first-century Western discourse, and it is possible to understand the appeal of conspiracy theories as in part a recognition of the intimacy between "terrorism" and "state terror." Paranoia, as many thinkers and writers have observed, shapes the very possibility of modernity's interpretation of itself. For a recent study, see John Farrell, *Paranoia and Modernity: Cervantes to Rousseau* (Ithaca: Cornell University Press, 2006).

13. Portions of this tape were broadcast by Al Jazeera on September 7, 2006.

14. Judith Butler, *Precarious Life: The Powers of Mourning and Violence* (London: Verso, 2004), 46. I have argued for a connection between nationalism and melancholia along slightly different lines in *The Politics of Aesthetics*.

15. The phrase "ground zero" has become extremely common in recent years and is now often used to denote the epicenter of natural disasters (e.g., New Orleans during Hurricane Katrina), but the military origins of the phrase bear keeping in mind. For some useful background, see http://en.wikipedia .org/wiki/Ground_zero. As it happens, until 2006 the Pentagon boasted at the center of its plaza a lunch canteen informally dubbed "Ground Zero Café" because, according to Cold War rumor, the Soviets had missiles targeting the structure, which they mistook for a bomb shelter. At present writing the building is being torn down and replaced with a more modern eatery.

16. Butler, *Precarious Life*, 41.

17. For a more literally Freudian argument that the term "Ground Zero" functions as a symptom or unconscious acknowledgment, within the American media apparatus, of guilt for the bombing of Hiroshima, see Gene Ray, "Ground Zero: Hiroshima Haunts 9/11," *Alternative Press Review*, http://www .altpr.org/modules.php?op = modload&name = News&file = article&sid = 8& mod.

18. Samuel Weber, *Targets of Opportunity: On the Militarization of Thinking* (New York: Fordham University Press, 2005). On the associated notion and praxis of "testing," see Avital Ronell, *The Test Drive* (Urbana: University of Illinois Press, 2005).

19. Rumsfeld's comment is reported by Richard Clarke in *Against All Enemies: Inside America's War on Terror* (New York: Free Press, 2004). I borrow the phrase "the politics of good intentions" from David Runciman, *The Politics of Good Intentions: History, Fear, and Hypocrisy in the New World Order* (Princeton: Princeton University Press, 2006); see esp. 31–53 for a fine analysis of Tony Blair's rhetoric, in particular. Here is Blair, speaking about the Kosovo conflict on April 28, 1999: "Whenever there are civilian casualties as a result of allied bombs, they are by error. We regret them, and we take precautions to avoid them. The people whom the Serb paramilitaries are killing are killed deliberately. That is the difference between us and them" (44). Examples of similar claims by U.S., Israeli, and other governments could be multiplied endlessly.

20. Donald Pease reads the figure of Ground Zero as a rekeying of an American myth of innocence—of the emptiness of the land prior to its settling—and thus of an ongoing effacement of the genocide of native populations. Ground Zero thus represents both a violation of a foundational myth and its perpetuation: "The state of emergency Bush erected at 'Ground Zero' was thereafter endowed with the responsibility to defend the 'Homeland' because the terrorists' violation of virgin land had alienated the national people from their imaginary way of inhabiting the nation." This substitution "drastically altered the national people's foundational fantasy about their relationship to the national territory, redefining it in terms of the longing of a dislocated population for their lost homeland" (Donald Pease, "American Literary Studies and American Cultural Studies in the Times of the National Emergency: J's Paradoxes," in *Provocations to Reading: J. Hillis Miller and the Democracy to Come*, ed. Barbara Cohen and Dragan Kujundžić [New York: Fordham University Press, 2005], 190–91). As I am about to make clear, I think Pease is right to link the figure of Ground Zero to that of the "Homeland"; but where he sees a "shift in dominant narratives from a secured, virgin nation to a violent, insecure state of emergency" (191) occurring in the Bush administration's response to the 9/11 attacks, I see not so much a shift to another narrative

as a heightening of ideological motifs and institutional practices that long pre-
date the attacks.

21. The reference here, of course, is to Heidegger's idiomatic account of
modern technics: *Ge-stell*, usually translated as "enframing," names a process
of extraction and stockpiling whereby the world is made into *Bestand*, "standing-reserve." Standing-reserve results from a process of objectification that has
gone so far that objects are no longer really objects, since they exist for the sake
of something else. See, among other texts, Martin Heidegger, "The Question
Concerning Technology," in *The Question Concerning Technology and Other
Essays*, trans. and ed. William Lovitt (New York: Harper Torchbooks, 1977),
3–35; for the German text, see *Vorträge und Aufsätze* (Tübingen: Gunther
Neske, 1954), 13–44.

22. See the next chapter for a developed version of this claim. See also, for
an interesting if, in my view, awkwardly dogmatic Heideggerian account of
the "war on terror," Andrew J. Mitchell, "Heidegger and Terrorism," *Research
in Phenomenology* 35 (2005): 181–218. Mitchell asserts that "the withdrawal of
being shows itself today in terrorism, where beings exist as terrorized," and
that "this 'ontological' point demands that there be the 'ontic' threat of real
terrorists" (182), but he never works to define or think through that loaded
term "terrorist." Nor is the metaphysical concept of the *era* put into question.
Since I have myself sought to think the "war on terror" as an expression of
techno-metaphysics, I am ready to agree with much of what Mitchell says, but
it is necessary both to move more carefully between levels of analysis (political,
technical, etc.) than he does and to read Heidegger more carefully and critically than he does. Mitchell represents the technical regime of *Ge-stell* as a total
accomplishment—an end of history in which "there is no longer any friction"
and "all uncertainty is lost" (191): he misses the crucial complication in Heidegger's thought, which is that techno-metaphysics produces uncertainty even
as it achieves its certainties. A more deconstructive reading of Heidegger
would have helped Mitchell avoid making overhasty aesthetic-nationalist
claims: e.g., "This bond of terror is at the same time the bond of citizenry, the
bond of the citizens of the homeland America" (199).

23. The peculiarly Teutonic-sounding word "Homeland" needs to be interpreted in relation to Ground Zero, as Pease suggests. It does not seem to me
that, prior to 9/11, an American administration would have promoted this
particular word, or that the American media would have found it palatable.

24. Ambivalent because there is no such thing as a pure "state of exception," either in theory or in practice. I offer an appreciation and critique of
Giorgio Agamben's influential writing on sovereignty and the state of exception in the next chapter; for Agamben's position, see esp. *Homo Sacer: Sovereign*

Power and Bare Life, trans. Daniel Heller-Roazen (Stanford: Stanford University Press, 1998). For an extremely interesting account of Al-Qaeda as itself a movement deeply marked by the deracinating forces of globalization, see Faisal Devji, *Landscapes of the Jihad: Militancy, Morality, Modernity* (Ithaca: Cornell University Press, 2005).

25. For a brilliant fictional meditation on the figure of the zero and its ambivalent transcendental powers, see Thomas Pynchon, *Gravity's Rainbow* (New York: Viking, 1973), whose first chapter is in fact titled "Beyond the Zero." Many years ago, I attempted a reading of the figure of the zero in Pynchon: see my "Pynchon's Postmodern Sublime," *PMLA* 104 (1989): 152–62.

26. This is one of Primo Levi's great themes: "At a distance of years one can today definitely affirm that the history of the Lagers has been written almost exclusively by those who, like myself, never fathomed them to the bottom. Those who did so did not return, or their capacity for observation was paralyzed by suffering and incomprehension" (Primo Levi, *The Drowned and the Saved*, trans. Raymond Rosenthal [New York: Vintage, 1989], 17). The literature in this field is vast; for a careful and wide-ranging consideration of and contribution to trauma and Holocaust studies, see Geoffrey Hartman, *The Longest Shadow: In the Aftermath of the Holocaust* (Bloomington: Indiana University Press, 1996).

27. See Friend, *Watching the World Change*, for a helpful account of the photographic and videographic record of 9/11. As flight American 11 approached, the French filmmaker Jules Naudet, who was shooting downtown, raised his video camera toward the roar of the jet and caught the plane slamming into the north tower; so did a tourist across the East River; and so did two unmanned Webcams set up by the Internet artist Wolfgang Staehle (Friend, 3). Jules and Gedeon Naudet later incorporated their video into a documentary, *9/11*, released in 2002.

28. David Levi Strauss, *Between the Eyes: Essays on Photography and Politics* (New York: Aperture, 2003), 184. He does not provide proof for this statement.

29. Extracts from the NORAD tapes, published by *Vanity Fair* in August 2006, may be heard and read at: http://www.vanityfair.com/politics/features/2006/08/norad200608.

30. Daniel Mendelson, "September 11 at the Movies," *The New York Review of Books* 53, no. 14 (2006): 43.

31. Slavoj Žižek, *Welcome to the Desert of the Real: Five Essays on September 11 and Related Dates* (London: Verso, 2002), 11.

32. In an eloquent essay, Tom Junod argues that "it was, at last, the sight of the jumpers that provided the corrective to those who insisted on saying that what they were witnessing was 'like a movie,' for this was an ending as unimaginable as it was unbearable" (Tom Junod, "The Falling Man," *Esquire*

140, no. 3 (September 2003), available on-line at: http://www.esquire.com/fea
tures/ESQ0903-SEP_FALLINGMAN. I shall say a bit more about the particularly charged representations of the so-called "jumpers" later.

33. See Lawrence Wright, *The Looming Tower: Al Qaeda and the Road to
9/11* (New York: Knopf, 2006). Bin Laden, however, has claimed that the basic
idea of attacking American buildings came from the Israeli bombing of Beirut.
I would not be misunderstood to be advancing here the absurd (and ethnocen-
tric) suggestion that Hollywood blockbusters "caused" the attacks. I am simply
noting that the blockbuster forms part of the shaping (that is, not simply "external") context within which a spectacular terrorist act of this sort is conceived
and performed.

34. Susan Sontag, *Regarding the Pain of Others* (New York: Picador,
2003), 22.

35. For the latest official position of the medical establishment on trauma
and post-traumatic stress disorder, see the American Psychiatric Association's
Diagnostic and Statistical Manual of Mental Disorders, 4th ed. (Washington,
D.C.: American Psychiatric Association, 2000). The definition of post-
traumatic stress disorder (PTSD) and the delimitation of what counts as a
traumatic experience (or "traumatic stressor") is still evolving. My understanding of trauma owes much to Cathy Caruth's powerful work: see esp. her intro-
ductions to *Trauma: Explorations in Memory*, ed. Cathy Caruth (Baltimore:
Johns Hopkins University Press, 1995), 3–12, 151–57.

36. Sontag, *Regarding the Pain of Others*, 21.

37. In the *Vanity Fair* account that accompanies the released excerpts of
tape, one of the interviewees, Major Nasypany, tells Michael Bronner, the *Vanity Fair* writer (who was also an associate producer for the film *United 93*),
"When they told me there was a hijack, my first reaction was 'Somebody
started the exercise early . . . I actually said out loud, 'The hijack's not supposed to be for another hour.'" The coincidence of military exercise and terrorist attack has of course been a boon to conspiracy theorists.

38. For an account of and riposte to some of these denunciations of theory,
relativism, irony, etc., see Stanley Fish, "Postmodern Warfare: The Ignorance
of Our Warrior Intellectuals," *Harper's Magazine*, July 2002, 33–40.

39. The *9/11 Commission Report* tells us that Khalid Sheikh Mohammed
had "a grandiose original plan" involving ten hijacked airplanes; he imagined
that he himself would "land the tenth plane at a U.S. airport and, after killing
all adult male passengers on board and alerting the media, deliver a speech
excoriating U.S. support for Israel, the Philippines, and repressive governments in the Arab world" (154). This claim, like much else in the *Report*,
simply reflects what a prisoner (in this case Khalid Sheikh Mohammed) told

his interrogators, but at the very least it offers one example among many of Al-Qaeda's media-savvy imagination.

40. Junod's "Falling Man" was one of four articles in the final running for the first Michael Kelly journalism award in 2004. For a sustained consideration of the "jumpers" in 9/11 discourse, see also the first chapter of Karen Engle's forthcoming *Visual Culture and 9/11: Mourning and the Making of History*. I am grateful to her for sharing her manuscript with me. Engle, drawing (as I too am doing) on Derrida's reflections on futurity as threat, suggests that the representations of jumpers offer a discomfiting representation of "death-on-the-way" (5), rendering grimly specific the death that, as Roland Barthes long ago pointed out, shadows and illuminates all photographic images. See Roland Barthes, *Camera Lucida: Reflections on Photography*, trans. Richard Howard (New York: Hill and Wang, 1981).

41. Ground Zero was classified as a crime scene, and no photographers or journalists were granted access except for Joel Meyerowitz, who, in the preface to his impressive photography collection *Aftermath*, records being stopped and harassed constantly by police and other officials, despite being in possession of a letter of authorization from the Museum of the City of New York. As noted in n. 11, above, Meyerowitz's book appeared at the same time as another book titled *Aftermath*, collecting the amateur and surreptitious photographs of a policeman, John Botte. One likes to imagine Botte waving away Meyerowitz before snapping a quick shot or two himself. *Quis custodiet ipsos custodes?*

42. Karen Engle plausibly suggests that the quasi-anthropomorphic towers came to substitute for the bodies of the victims, so many of which had been annihilated or utterly fragmented, and were in most cases forbidden objects of media representation.

43. Sontag, *Regarding the Pain of Others*, 69. Questions of decorum intersect here with technologies and practices of censorship, in the first instance military censorship, as both Levi Strauss and Sontag remark. Levi Strauss recalls the U.S. military's press blackouts in Grenada, Panama, Iraq, and Afghanistan, and notes that, in the latter case, the military not only tightly controlled access but even purchased exclusive rights to commercial satellite imagery in order to shut down information flow (*Between the Eyes*, 190). Efforts to censor information, of course, have accompanied the mediatization of modern warfare since the Crimean War, as Sontag notes. Photography at the front was controlled severely during World War I and more erratically during World War II. Vietnam, the first televised war, was more loosely censored by U.S. military forces than were previous or subsequent wars.

44. See esp. my *Politics of Aesthetics*.

45. The first quotation derives from a considerably more complex sentence and discussion in Theodor W. Adorno, "Cultural Criticism and Society," in

Prisms, trans. Samuel Weber and Shierry Weber (Cambridge: MIT Press, 1967), 34. Lifted from its context and transformed into a sound bite of the intellectual-culture industry, this quotation offers a deeply misleading simplification of Adorno's aesthetic. My point here is simply that this phrase has become a commonplace for a reason.

46. The most publicized case is that of Eric Fischl's sculpture *Tumbling Woman*, briefly on display at Rockefeller Center before being withdrawn after much vociferous protest: see Junod, "Falling Man," for a vivid account and Engle, *Visual Culture and 9/11*, for a more sustained analysis. Junod's claim that representations of the "jumpers" sparked particularly fierce controversy in the United States is borne out not just by this case but also by that of Sharon Paz's cutouts of falling bodies titled *Falling*, briefly displayed and then removed from the Jamaica Center for the Arts.

47. Stockhausen's comment was published in *Die Zeit*, September 16, 2001: "Was da geschehen ist, ist—jetzt müssen Sie alle Ihr Gehirn umstellen—das grösste Kunstwerk, das es je gegeben hat [What happened there is—now you must all turn your brains around—the greatest artwork that there has ever been].") The source was a Norddeutscher Rundfunk tape transcript of a press conference (I thank Kate Bloodgood for tracking down this fact for me; I haven't been able to access the original recording), and Stockhausen has insisted that his remarks were quoted out of context and distorted. Whatever the truth of the matter, this affair exemplifies the force with which sound bites about 9/11 were created in the media in the weeks following the attacks. For Baudrillard's remark, see his *The Spirit of Terrorism and Other Essays*, trans. Chris Turner (London: Verso, 2002), 41.

48. Frank Lentricchia and Jody McAuliffe, *Crimes of Art and Terror* (Chicago: University of Chicago Press, 2003), 13, 12.

49. Hence the long-standing discomfort with "aesthetic" composition in documentary photography: for nonsimplifying discussion; see Levi Strauss, *Between the Eyes*, 3–11 passim, and Sontag, *Regarding the Pain of Others*, esp. 74–82. Sontag discusses the marked avoidance of artistry and professionalism in the *Here Is New York* show: "For the photography of atrocity, people want the weight of witnessing without the taint of artistry, which is equated with insincerity or mere contrivance" (26).

50. Bruno Bosteels has drawn my attention to a relevant debate between cultural critics Willy Thayer and Nelly Richard, which turns on the question of whether avant-garde aesthetics shares any ideological ground with the military coup that overthrew Salvador Allende on September 11, 1973. The texts are collected in *Pensamiento de los confines* 15 (December 2004): Willy Thayer, "El golpe como consumación de la vanguardia," 9–16; Nelly Richard, "Lo político y lo crítico en el arte: 'Quien teme a la neovanguardia?'" 17–28; Willy

Thayer, "Critica, nihilismo, e interrupción: La Avanzada después de Márgenes e Institución," 41.

51. Plotinus, *Enneads* 1.6.4. Plotinus recalls here the "shudder" that, according to Plato, the lover experiences when seeing for the first time the beautiful boy of his desiring (*Phaedrus*, 251a). The Greek word used by Plotinus that I am translating as "shock" here, *ekplēxis*, often means "terror."

52. Edmund Burke, *A Philosophical Enquiry into the Origin of Our Ideas of the Sublime and the Beautiful*, ed. James T. Boulton (1958; Notre Dame: University of Notre Dame Press, 1986), 107–8.

53. Adorno, *Aesthetic Theory*, trans. Robert Hullot-Kentor (Minneapolis: University of Minnesota Press, 1997), 47. In modernity, archaic terror becomes the shock experience: "Under patient contemplation artworks begin to move. To this extent they are truly afterimages of the primordial shudder in the age of reification: the terror of that age is recapitulated vis-à-vis reified objects" (79). Elsewhere in this text Adorno writes that "terror itself peers out of the eyes of beauty" (52) and proposes that art is linked to "the shudder [*Schauer*] of the new" (20) and to "explosion" (84). A more extensive reading of Adorno on art and shock would also have to take up his inflection of the ancient topos of philosophy as the experience of wonder: "in philosophy we experience a shock: the deeper, the more vigorous its penetration, the greater our suspicion that philosophy removes us from things as they are" (Adorno, *Negative Dialectics*, trans. E. B. Ashton [New York: Continuum, 1973], 364).

54. I have written at greater length on aesthetic shock and the unstable relationship between art and kitsch in "Island Mysteries," my afterword to James Elkins, ed., *Art History Versus Aesthetics* (New York: Routledge, 2005), 269–90. The literature on the "postmodern sublime" is considerable. See my "Pynchon's Postmodern Sublime" for a critique of the most influential text in this mini-genre—the text that became the first chapter of and gave its title to Fredric Jameson's *Postmodernism; or, The Cultural Logic of Late Capitalism* (Durham, N.C.: Duke University Press, 1991). Earlier versions of Jameson's chapter were published as essays at various points in the 1980s; the most influential version—the version to which I refer in my 1989 article—appeared in *New Left Review* 146 (1984): 53–92. See also Jean-François Lyotard, *The Postmodern Condition: A Report on Knowledge*, trans. Geoffrey Bennington and Brian Massumi (Minneapolis: University of Minnesota Press, 1984).

55. It is not at all clear what we are doing when we imagine our own death (if that is indeed what we are doing) when faced with spectacles of ruin. A certain textual and technical element persists at such moments, as deconstructive readings of the sublime have shown and as I shall be suggesting here. So, however, does a transcendental impulse. (I shall say a little more about religion later in the present essay.) As Thomas Weiskel claims in the opening sentence

of his great study: "The essential claim of the sublime is that human beings can, in feeling and speech, transcend the human" (*The Romantic Sublime: Studies in the Structure and Psychology of Transcendence* [Baltimore: Johns Hopkins University Press, 1976], 3). The sublime plays an extremely complex and vexed role in Kant's Third *Critique*; for a rigorous survey of some late-twentieth-century scholarship on this topic, see Peter Fenves, "Taking Stock of the Kantian Sublime," *Eighteenth-Century Studies* 28, no. 1 (1994): 65–82.

56. I am referring to Martin Heidegger, "Die Zeit des Weltbildes," in *Holzwege* (Frankfurt am Main: Vittorio Klostermann, 1950), 69–104; "The Age of the World Picture," in *The Question Concerning Technology and Other Essays*, 115–54. Because Heidegger's vocabulary presents special challenges, I give page numbers German/English in what follows. The essay dates from 1938.

57. Guy Debord, *The Society of the Spectacle*, trans. Donald Nicholson-Smith (New York: Zone Books, 1995), 26. For a powerful elaboration of the dislocating effects of spectacle and theatricality, see Samuel Weber, *Theatricality as Medium* (New York: Fordham University Press, 2004). I am indebted to his discussion of Debord and theatricality in the context of 9/11 (326–35). See also his prescient remark that "the immediate destruction produced images that will haunt us for many years but will also become what Freud calls 'screen memories,' blotting out many of the relations that contributed to the actual events, without which they become speciously transparent" (358).

58. In a similar spirit, Derrida, writing of "the colossal" in Kant, reflects on "the cise of the colossus" as "perhaps, between the presentable and the unpresentable, the passage from the one to the other as much as the irreducibility of the one to the other" (Jacques Derrida, *The Truth in Painting*, trans. Geoffrey Bennington and Ian McLeod [Chicago: University of Chicago Press, 1987], 143).

59. The film industry's nervous relationship to 9/11 has frequently been noted. Some films (most famously an Arnold Schwarzenegger vehicle, *Collateral Damage*) had their release dates set back after 9/11; others (most famously, *Men in Black* 2) were partly reshot to avoid featuring the World Trade Center; a Jackie Chan film, *Nosebleed*, about foiling a plot to blow up the WTC, was cancelled; etc.

60. To the point that, unlike all the other characters in *World Trade Center*, he refuses to tender a first name when asked, insisting on "Staff Sergeant Karns." He wanders Ground Zero calling out, "We're marines! You are our mission!" and when help arrives he offers a paramedic his "Marine K-bar" super-knife as the only tool up to the task. At such moments it is impossible to tell what the film wants us to think of its own cornball dialogue—or of Karns himself, who (like the protagonists of a certain familiar kind of Hollywood film: *Taxi Driver*, *Rambo*) moves in the gray area between nutcase and

movie hero (the hero of a Western: the John Wayne figure who heals the family and community and moves on).

61. The best place to begin a consideration of the sacred and the sublime is with Marjorie Hope Nicolson's classic study *Mountain Gloom and Mountain Glory: The Development of the Aesthetics of the Infinite* (Ithaca: Cornell University Press, 1959), which argues that the seventeenth-century invention of the natural sublime—the sublime of mountains, waterfalls, etc.—represents a transfer of divine attributes (e.g., infinitude, oneness) from God to Newtonian space and thence to landscapes.

62. See Samuel P. Huntington, *The Clash of Civilizations and the Remaking of World Order* (New York: Simon and Schuster, 1996).

63. Derrida, for one, has argued that "the imperturbable and interminable development of critical and technoscientific reason, far from opposing religion, bears, supports, and supposes it." See "Faith and Knowledge: The Two Sources of 'Religion' at the Limits of Reason Alone," trans. Samuel Weber, in *Religion*, ed. Jacques Derrida and Gianni Vattimo (Stanford: Stanford University Press, 1998), 28. This dense, important essay explores the possibility that "religion and reason have the same source"; they "develop in tandem, drawing from this common resource: the testimonial pledge of every performative, committing it to respond as much before the other as for the high-performance performativity of technoscience" (ibid.). The result is an unsteady and violent complicity between faith and enlightenment: "religion today allies itself with tele-technoscience, to which it reacts with all its forces" (46). An emphasis on the fundamental persistence of the religious is also a feature of psychoanalytic theory, particularly in its Lacanian form. For a lucid exposition, see Kenneth Reinhard and Julia Reinhard Lupton, "The Subject of Religion: Lacan and the Ten Commandments," *Diacritics* 33, no. 2 (2003): 71–97: "In Lacan's analysis, it is not that secular intellectuals suffer from unexamined religious 'suppositions' or assumptions, to be swept away through a little ideology-critique or time on the couch. The case is rather, in Lacan's strong formulation, that religious discourse *supposes us*—supports and underwrites our very structures of being, subjectivity, and social interaction" (71). For an important collection of essays focused on the issues I am highlighting, see Hent de Vries and Samuel Weber, eds., *Religion and Media* (Stanford: Stanford University Press, 2001).

64. But not the religious idiom, at least not entirely. As the film begins we hear the future hijackers praying in Arabic; as daylight comes they head for the airport past a "God Bless America" sign: a visual counter to the Islamic prayers. The monotheisms are at war.

65. *United 93* was strenuously marketed and largely received as a "memorial." As the film critic Dennis Lim noted upon its release, it "was famously made with the support of the passengers' families, the press kit includes bios

not of the actors but of the people they portray, and Universal is donating 10 percent of the first weekend gross to the Flight 93 memorial fund" (Dennis Lim, "A Flight to Remember," *Village Voice*, April 18, 2006: http://www .villagevoice.com/film/0616,lim,72901,20.html).

66. Lim observes that this dedication replaces the title card with which the film was screened in pre-release, " America's war on terror had begun." This is not the only way in which the film indulges in a bellicose, apocalyptic tone. Its celebration of resistance slides imperturbably into the same aggressive-nationalistic idiom in which Stone's *World Trade Center* indulges. Not all the families of the victims cooperated in the making of *United 93*, and it has been suggested that the film's slanderous portrayal of German businessman Christian Adams as a Eurowimp who counsels appeasement—who even rises to betray the uprising of the passengers and has to be forcibly quelled by the Americans—was facilitated and perhaps even inspired by his family's unwillingness to cooperate with the filmmaker. But it is equally likely that the film's ideological vision required this formulaic bit of nastiness.

67. Sontag, *Regarding the Pain of Others*, 110.

68. Sontag has just named Baudrillard as the extreme representative of a brand of theorizing that seems "a French specialty": "Jean Baudrillard . . . claims to believe that images, simulated realities, are all that exist now" (ibid., 109). Simpson, in *9/11*, over the course of his fine discussion of theory in relation to September 11, argues for a more nuanced understanding of Baudrillard's project. Discussing the provocative title and argument of Baudrillard's book about the "first" Gulf War, *The Gulf War Did Not Take Place*, trans. Paul Patton (Bloomington: Indiana University Press, 1995), Simpson remarks that "Baudrillard's point is a serious one. The war was conducted by and represented to the victors as if it were a glorified computer game directed by remote control from afar and involving no American casualties worth listing" (129; see 129–30 for the full discussion).

69. Jacques Derrida, *Specters of Marx: The State of the Debt, the Work of Mourning, and the New International*, trans. Peggy Kamuf (New York: Routledge, 1994), 85.

70. Derrida, "Autoimmunity," 93.

71. Ibid., 101.

72. Baudrillard, *Spirit of Terrorism*, 51, 38–39, 7.

73. Ibid., 7.

74. Derrida identifies three moments or versions of autoimmunity. (1) The threat comes from the "inside": the terrorists exploited the technology, etc. of the superpower and guarantor of world order in attacking the symbolic "head" of that order. (2) The threat, though a Cold War legacy, comes from the "future" as the traumatic possibility of a worse disaster to come. (3) The

threat is exacerbated by efforts to defend against it. See Derrida, "Autoimmunity," 94–100.

II. WAR ON TERROR

1. Bob Woodward, *Bush at War* (New York: Simon and Schuster, 2002), 46.

2. Bush's first words to Dick Cheney on the morning of September 11, according to Woodward, were "We're at war" (ibid., 17). Sentences about being at war were drafted for Bush for his evening statement on September 11; wanting a more reassuring message, the president ordered them struck out, even though the phrase "reflected what Bush had been saying all day to the NSC [National Security Council] and his staff" (30). A day later, however, in his 11 A.M. newsbriefing on September 12, Bush resurrected the elided sentences: "The deliberate and deadly attacks which were carried out yesterday against our country were more than acts of terror. They were acts of war." (cited in ibid., 45).

3. Jean Bodin, *On Sovereignty: Four Chapters from the Six Books of the Commonwealth*, trans. Julian H. Franklin (Cambridge: Cambridge University Press, 1992), 1, 10. The original French edition of Bodin's *Les six livres de la république* dates from 1576. Thomas Hobbes, in *Leviathan* (1651), cuts the Gordian knot by identifying sovereignty with the very promulgation of law and affirming that "the Sovereign Power, whether placed in One Man, as in Monarchy, or in one Assembly of men, as in Popular and Aristocratic Commonwealths, is as great as possibly men can be imagined to make it" (*Leviathan*, ed. C. B. Macpherson [Harmondsworth: Penguin, 1985], 260). Even in Hobbes, however, there are complications, for the sovereign cannot absorb into himself the fundamentals of natural law. Since "the Obligation of Subjects to the Soveraign is understood to last as long, and no longer, than the power lasteth, by which he is able to protect them," the Hobbesian sovereign remains radically exposed to contingency in the form of natural law, i.e., "the right men have by Nature to protect themselves, when no one else can protect them, [a right that] can by no Covenant be relinquished" (272).

4. For an interesting if, of course, highly opinionated survey of the Western traditions of sovereignty, war, and law from antiquity through the twentieth century, see Carl Schmitt, *The Nomos of the Earth in the International Law of the Jus Publicum Europaeum*, trans. G. L. Ulmen (New York: Telos Press, 2006).

5. Jean-Luc Nancy, "War, Law, Sovereignty—Technê," in *Rethinking Technologies*, ed. Verena Andermatt Conley (Minneapolis: University of Minnesota Press, 1993), 29, italics in the original.

6. Judith Butler, *Precarious Life: The Powers of Mourning and Violence* (London: Verso, 2004), 52. Butler draws here on Michel Foucault, "Governmentality," in *The Foucault Effect: Studies in Governmentality*, ed. Graham Burchell, Colin Gordon, and Peter Miller (Chicago: University of Chicago Press, 1991), 87–104.

7. Jacques Derrida, "Autoimmunity: Real and Symbolic Suicides," in Giovanna Borradori, *Philosophy in a Time of Terror: Dialogues with Jürgen Habermas and Jacques Derrida* (Chicago: University of Chicago Press, 2003), 93.

8. I am seeking to describe a particular postmodern predicament in these pages, but of course the motif of the fearful sovereign is an ancient one. Xenophon tells us that the tyrant has "a soul distracted by fears," seeing and fearing enemies everywhere precisely because everyone fears him. (Thus, "as if there were a perpetual war on, [tyrants] are compelled to support an army or perish.") Xenophon, *Hiero or Tyrannicus*, 6.5 and 4.11, quoted in the translation provided in Leo Strauss, *On Tyranny* (1963; Ithaca: Cornell University Press, 1975).

9. Walter Benjamin, "Critique of Violence," in *Reflections: Essays, Aphorisms, Autobiographical Writings*, trans. Edmund Jephcott (New York: Schocken Books, 1978), 277–300.

10. The quotation is attributed to a suspect in the Bali bombing of October 2002, as reported by the *New York Times*: "At least one suspect has said that the Bali attacks were meant to hurt 'America and its allies because they are international terrorists'" ("Indonesia Bombing Kills at Least 10 in Midday Attack," *The New York Times*, Wednesday, August 6, 2003, A1). Though I don't pretend to have conducted a proper empirical survey of contemporary usage, my sense is that one almost never encounters the words "terrorism" or "terrorist" being used as affirmative labels by contributors to the mainstream media.

11. The allusion here, of course, is to Carl Schmitt's epigrammatic definition of sovereignty in the opening sentence of *Political Theology*: "Sovereign is he who decides on the exception" (*Political Theology: Four Chapters on the Concept of Sovereignty*, trans. George Schwab [Cambridge: MIT Press, 1985]).

12. Bush's statement comes from a speech on September 20, 2001, as cited in Woodward, *Bush at War*, 108. For the remarks by Cheney and Rumsfeld, my source is "After the Attacks: The White House; Bush Warns of a Wrathful, Shadowy and Inventive War," *The New York Times*, Monday, September 17, 2001, A2. Bush's characterization of the war on terror as a "crusade" (a pseudo-gaffe that was, of course, also a message to his religious base) dates from September 12. "Operation Infinite Justice" was the original title of the Pentagon's Afghanistan operation, later retitled "Operation Enduring Freedom." The phrase "axis of evil," describing North Korea, Iraq, and Iran, was launched over the course of a presidential address on January 29, 2002.

13. See Walter Benjamin, "Die Waffen von Morgen: Schlagen mit Chlora-zetophenol, Diphenylaminchlorasin und Dichloräthylsulfid" (1925), in *Gesammelte Schriften*, (Frankfurt am Main: Suhrkamp, 1980), IV, 1.2, 473–76. Benjamin's speculations concern the intangible notion of a "front" in the case of sophisticated chemical warfare.

14. The War Powers Act of 1973 affirms the president's sovereignty insofar as he decides—at least to some extent—on the exception: "The constitutional powers of the President as Commander-in-Chief to introduce United States Armed Forces into hostilities, or into situations where imminent involvement in hostilities is clearly indicated by the circumstances, are exercised only pursuant to (1) a declaration of war, (2) specific statutory authorization, or (3) a national emergency created by attack upon the United States, its territories or possessions, or its armed forces" (War Powers Act, sec. 2. [c]). Bush had the right to respond in sovereign (though limited and local) fashion to what was certainly a "national emergency" on September 11, 2001. The Bush administration subsequently, under the provisos of the War Powers Act, sought and obtained statutory authorizations for military action against Afghanistan (or, more precisely, against "those nations, organizations, or persons [the president] determines planned, authorized, committed, or aided the terrorist attacks that occurred on September 11, 2001, or harbored such organizations or persons") in 2001 and against Iraq in 2002.

15. Resistance fighters, guerrillas, and "subversives" have often been labeled "terrorists" by governments and occupying powers throughout much of the twentieth century. The rise of Marxist-inspired terrorist groups in the West in the 1960s obviously gave this term a boost: it circulated visibly during the military repressions of the 1970s in Argentina, Uruguay, Chile, and Brazil, for instance. The earliest appearance in the United States of the specific phrase "war on terrorism" that my research assistant, Mary Powell, and I have been able to find is in the title of a *Newsweek* article from October 1977, "The New War on Terrorism." But the notion of war overlaps with that of terror in much Vietnam-era war reporting (the Viet Cong are terrorists, purveyors of terror, etc.), while the first governmental agency focused on the "terrorist" threat per se, created in the wake of the Munich Olympics of 1972, was the Cabinet Committee to Combat Terrorism. There are many studies of the history of (the notion of) terrorism and of terrorism's link to mass media. For a long-range perspective, see Jeffory A. Clymer, *America's Culture of Terrorism: Violence, Capitalism, and the Written Word* (Chapel Hill: University of North Carolina Press, 2003); for a study more focused on the 1970s to the present, see Melani McAlister, "A Cultural History of the War Without End," in *History and September 11th*, ed. Joanne Meyerowitz (Philadelphia: Temple University Press, 2003), 94–116.

16. Brief of amicus curiae, American Center for Law and Justice, in support of petitioners in the matter of *Donald H. Rumsfeld, et al., Petitioners, v. José Padilla, et al., Respondents*, Supreme Court case No. 03–1027, 8.

17. The present essay is not set up to weigh this question—for my purposes here it suffices simply to ask it, as a way of suggesting the nonobviousness of the shape and extent of the "war on terror." The question obviously turns on the problem of what differences ought to be regarded as "fundamental" ones. That the Bush administration has indulged in more violent displays of sovereignty than its precursors (or, one hopes, its successors)—withdrawing from the Anti-Ballistic Missile Treaty and the Kyoto Protocol; rejecting and undermining the International Criminal Court; unilaterally launching what a different U.S. leadership probably would have judged, on pragmatic grounds, an unnecessary invasion of Iraq; shamelessly affirming its right to torture and arbitrary detain suspects; etc.—has certainly resulted in the temporary alienation of First World allies and has probably resulted in more death and destruction than previous post-Vietnam U.S. administrations can claim to have accomplished directly. Small ideological differences can have considerable impact on the world when so much power is wielded by a single government. The question remains, however, whether the Bush administration's unilateralism and bellicosity adds up to a "fundamental" shift in U.S. foreign policy; for arguments to the contrary, see the many books and other writings of Noam Chomsky, esp. *Rogue States: The Rule of Force in World Affairs* (Cambridge, Mass.: South End Press, 2000). Jacques Derrida reminds us that "as early as 1993, Clinton, after coming to power, in effect inaugurated the politics of retaliation and sanction against rogue states by declaring in an address to the United Nations that his country would make use whenever it deemed it appropriate of article 51, that is, of the article of exception, and that the United States would act 'multilaterally when possible, but unilaterally when necessary'" (*Rogues: Two Essays on Reason*, trans. Pascale-Anne Brault and Michael Naas [Stanford: Stanford University Press, 2005], 103). (Article 51 recognizes a state's right to defend itself if attacked.)

18. J. L. Austin, *How to Do Things with Words*, 2d ed., ed. J. O. Urmson and Marina Sbisà (Oxford: Oxford University Press, 1980), 21.

19. I cannot, of course, even begin to suggest in a footnote the ramifications of the Bush administration's actions (to remain only within that context) during its disastrous eight years. (Year eight is, in any case, still in course as I write these lines.) The legal consequences of Bush's nonlegal but presidential pronouncements are of particular interest here, since one is able to observe firsthand the transformation of an ambiguous figure (the "declaration" of war on terror) and a complex political process (Congress granting the president the right to perform certain military actions, etc.) into a literal affirmation of

presidential "wartime powers" in the courts. (For one relatively restrained example among many, see the arguments before the Supreme Court in *Rasul et al. v. Bush, President of the United States, et al.* [No. 03–334; argued April 20, 2004; decided June 28, 2004], particularly Justice Scalia's dissent. For more full-throated affirmations of the president's near-infinite wartime powers, see the American Center for Law and Justice's brief of amicus curiae, cited earlier, for the Supreme Court case *Donald H. Rumsfeld et al., Petitioners, v. José Padilla, et al., Respondents* [No. 03–1027].) Of the president's many efforts to expand the sovereign powers of his office ("signing statements" that nullify laws he is reluctantly signing, a ferocious attention to secrecy, etc.), probably the most egregious and widely discussed has been his affirmation of the sovereign's right to torture terrorists. The notorious "torture" brief drawn up for President Bush by administration lawyers in March 2003 based its claim on sovereign exception: "in order to respect the president's inherent constitutional authority to manage a military campaign," prohibition against torture "must be construed as inapplicable to interrogation undertaken pursuant to his commander-in-chief authority": see "Working Group Report on Detainee Interrogations in the Global War on Terrorism: Assessment of Legal, Historical, Policy, and Operational Considerations," March 6, 2003, available on various Internet sites. Relevant documents are now collected in Mark Danner, *Torture and Truth: America, Abu Ghraib, and the War on Terror* (New York: New York Review Books, 2004). Many books have since appeared detailing the Bush administration's investment in torture: for one of the most up-to-date accounts available at present writing, see Philippe Sands, *Torture Team: Rumsfeld's Memo and the Betrayal of American Values* (New York: Palgrave, 2008). (The title references a memo Rumsfeld signed on December 2, 2002, authorizing the interrogation "techniques" that have since become famous—waterboarding, sexual humiliation, etc.)

20. J. Hillis Miller, *Speech Acts in Literature* (Stanford: Stanford University Press, 2001), 28.

21. Miller's wonderful summary reads in part: "In Austin's examples Murphy's law is abundantly obeyed. What can go wrong does go wrong. People marry monkeys. Horses are appointed consul. British warships are christened the *Generalissimo Stalin* by some 'low type' who happens to come by. Someone is tempted not to eat an apple, as Adam was tempted by Eve to do, but to have another whack of ice cream, perhaps even more unhealthy than the Edenic apple. Patients in lunatic asylums are boiled alive. The purser rather than the captain tries to marry people on shipboard. Someone in a football game breaks the rules by picking up the ball and running with it, thereby inventing rugby. Monkeys utter the command 'Go!' Donkeys are shot. Cats are drowned in butter. Dogs or penguins are baptized. The command is given 'Shoot her!' A

ferocious bull paws the field, ready to charge, or a thunderstorm threatens, and all you can do is shout 'Bull!' or 'Thunder!' People bequeath objects they do not own" (50).

22. I have tried my hand at explaining why and how the idea of "literary theory" arose in a particularly American institutional context in "Aesthetics, Theory, and the Profession of Literature: Derrida and Romanticism," *Studies in Romanticism* 46, no. 2 (2007): 227 46.

23. Giorgio Agamben, *Homo Sacer: Sovereign Power and Bare Life*, trans. Daniel Heller-Roazen (Stanford: Stanford University Press, 1998), 174.

24. Much of Agamben's thinking in this section of *Homo Sacer* bears the imprint of Hannah Arendt's incisive meditations on statelessness in *The Origins of Totalitarianism* (1951; New York: Harvest, 1994): see esp. 266–302, where Arendt takes up the paradox that "a man who is nothing but a man has lost the very qualities which make it possible for other people to treat him as a man" (300). As I shall review later in this chapter, what Agamben will call "bare life" Arendt calls "natural givenness" (302), "the abstract nakedness of being nothing but human" (300). Agamben's claim to have discovered a difference between Aristotle's use of the words *zoē* and *bios* also bears some resemblance to some of Arendt's reflections in *The Human Condition* (1958; Chicago: University of Chicago Press, 1998); see esp. 12–15.

25. Derrida, *Rogues*, 101.

26. The charade of the United States granting "sovereignty" to Iraq in the early summer of 2004 offers a good example of the way in which sovereignty exploits its own nominal self-curtailing—and also a good example of the wider ambiguities and contingencies within which even a superpower is forced to operate (it being obvious both that the United States intended to continue to control Iraq as thoroughly as possible through military means and that the United States was not sufficiently in control of Iraq to make good political theater out of the "handover" of sovereignty). I'll take time out for an anecdote. As reported by media (my source is the *Los Angeles Times*, June 29, 2004, A10, "A Brief Note Upends NATO Summit in Istanbul"), Bush was passed a note by Condoleezza Rice: "Mr. President, Iraq is sovereign. Letter was passed from Bremer at 10:26 AM Iraq time—Condi." Bush scrawled on the note: "Let Freedom Reign!" The idea of freedom reigning rather than ringing is a nice touch, unintended by the president, one imagines, but appropriate to the fictionality and ambiguity of Iraqi "sovereignty."

27. See *Rasul et al. v. Bush*, 5 (per the pagination of the case at the FindLaw Web site). The concurring opinion of Justice Kennedy specifies that "Guantanamo Bay is in every practical respect a United States territory" and that "this lease is no ordinary lease" (9). Justice Scalia's dissent insists, on the contrary,

that "Guantanamo Bay is not a sovereign domain, and even if it were, jurisdiction would be limited to subjects" (14).

28. The relationship between secrecy and the exercise of sovereign power in the postwar national-security state deserves consideration here. It has become a presumption of modern life that the executive branch and its intelligence agencies engage in activities that are not simply "above the law" but illegitimate—so much so that criminal prosecution might be a danger if certain actions were brought to light. The fiercely secretive Bush administration has of course taken this aspect of executive power, like all others, to an extreme. There has been much good writing about Guantánamo as a site of sovereign exception: see esp. Judith Butler's subtle and moving chapter "Infinite Detention" in *Precarious Life*, 50–100.

29. At times this excessive character of sovereignty comes through in Agamben's analysis, as in his discussion of Benjamin's notion (in "Critique of Violence") of "divine violence" as a more-than-sovereign violence "situated in a zone in which it is no longer possible to distinguish between exception and rule" (*Homo Sacer*, 65), but even here Agamben fails to emphasize the uncertain status of sovereign violence (which maintains "the link between violence and law even at the point of their indistinction," as opposed to divine violence, which is "the dissolution of the link between violence and law"; ibid.). Throughout his study, Agamben intermittently downplays the fundamental contamination afflicting concepts such as "sovereignty" or "bare life"; his ungenerous remarks about Derrida's work and his misrepresentation of "deconstruction" (54) are no doubt in this respect symptomatic.

30. Rationalistic accounts of terrorism are of course well represented within the U.S. military, U.S. government agencies, and associated organizations in the private sector and the universities. For an example of the sort of technocratic-pragmatic advice being offered, see Louise Richardson, *What Terrorists Want: Understanding the Enemy, Containing the Threat* (New York: Random House, 2006).

31. Doyne Dawson, *The Origins of Western Warfare: Militarism and Morality in the Ancient World* (Boulder, Colo.: Westview Press, 1996), 13. On the *jus publicum Europaeum*, see Schmitt, *Nomos*.

32. With "the bracketing of war, European humanity had achieved something extraordinary: renunciation of the criminalization of the opponent, and thus the relativization of enmity, the negation of absolute enmity. That really was an extraordinary, even an incredibly human accomplishment, that men renounced a discrimination and denigration of the enemy" (Carl Schmitt, *Theory of the Partisan: Intermediate Commentary on the Concept of the Political*, trans. G. L. Ulmen [New York: Telos Press, 2007], 90, translation slightly modified). Schmitt develops this theme in various texts and contexts, and notes

that a bracketing of (intra-Christian) war was also accomplished by the medieval Christian order (see *Nomos*, 58, passim).

33. Paul Virilio, *Pure War* (New York: Semiotext[e], 1983), 26. Like so many voices within the modern Western tradition, Virilio places war at the origin of politics, though he does not make clear whether the city constitutes itself in war or whether war constitutes itself in the city: on the one hand, "the city is the result of war" (3); on the other hand, "when the State was constituted, it developed war as an organization, as territorial economy, as economy of capitalization, of technology" (4). Ever since World War I, Virilio suggests, we have been living in a permanent wartime economy, and ever since the development of the possibility of nuclear war, we have been living in what Virilio paradoxically calls "pure war": an endless deferral of war by way of an endless militarization of life, all conducted under the shadow of a pure war that would be fought by machines ("Pure War no longer needs men, and that's why it's pure"; 171).

34. John Arquilla and David Ronfeldt, *Networks and Netwars* (Santa Monica, Calif.: RAND, 2001), 2, as cited and discussed in Samuel Weber, *Targets of Opportunity: On the Militarization of Thinking* (New York: Fordham University Press, 2005). Weber is interested in the complexities of "netwar" (a mode of conflict in which the combatants are organized into nets of horizontal relationships, without "heads" that can be targeted easily), but he points out that so long as *targeting* persists, an effort to limit and control indeterminacy still remains. Targeting is binary (you hit or you miss); thus, Weber concludes, RAND-type speculations remain driven by a doomed effort to control the future and strip death of its terrors.

35. Schmitt writes presciently of the "revolutionary partisan" as "the true central figure of war," though he has in mind the Maoist revolutionary rather than the religiously motivated terrorist (*Theory of the Partisan*, 30). The revolutionary partisan is to be distinguished from the territorially racinated, "telluric," or true partisan. Absolute war results from the criminalization of the enemy: "if the war as a whole is fought with criminalizations of opponents . . . the ultimate goal is destruction of the enemy state's government; then the revolutionary disruption of criminalization of the enemy follows in such a way that the partisan becomes the true hero of war. He enforces the death penalty against the criminal, and, if the tables are turned, risks being treated as a criminal or parasite. That is the logic of a war of *justa causa* [just cause] without recognition of a *justus hostis* [just enemy]. Thereby, the revolutionary partisan becomes the true central figure of war."

36. George Orwell, *Nineteen Eighty-Four* (New York: Harcourt, Brace, 1949), 5, passim. "War is Peace" is one of the three slogans of the Party (the

other two are "Freedom is Slavery" and "Ignorance is Strength"). My reference to Kant is to his famous essay "On Perpetual Peace": Immanuel Kant, *Perpetual Peace and Other Essays*, trans. Ted Humphrey (Indianapolis: Hackett, 1983), 106–39.

37. "Even in a fully civilized society there remains this superior esteem for the warrior. . . . . Hence, no matter how much people may dispute, when they compare the statesman with the general, as to which one deserves the superior respect, an aesthetic judgement decides in favor of the general. Even war has something sublime about it if it is carried out in an orderly way and with respect for the sanctity of the citizens' rights" (Immanuel Kant, *Critique of Judgment*, trans. Werner S. Pluhar [Indianapolis: Hackett, 1987], 121–22). The affects or themes of sublimity and glory can easily be granted pathetic or existential dimensions. Cormac McCarthy gives fine voice to a nihilistic, pseudo-Nietzschean version of war's sublimity in *Blood Meridian* in one of the terrible Judge Holden's speeches: "This is the nature of war, whose stake is at once the game and the authority and the justification. Seen so, war is the truest form of divination. It is the testing of one's will and the will of another within that larger will which because it binds them is therefore forced to select. War is the ultimate game because war is at last a forcing of the unity of existence. War is god" (*Blood Meridian, or The Evening Redness in the West* [1985; New York: Vintage, 1992], 249).

38. I have studied the figure of "the body" at some length in *The Politics of Aesthetics: Nationalism, Gender, Romanticism* (Stanford: Stanford University Press, 2003), 74–94, passim.

39. Samuel Weber, "Wartime," in *Violence, Identity, and Self-Determination*, ed. Hent de Vries and Samuel Weber (Stanford: Stanford University Press, 1997), 99. This rich essay is necessary reading for anyone interested in the rhetorical and epistemological complexity of the notion of "war." The fact that, in an essay originally written in 1994, Weber is able to predict that "the isolated act of terrorism becomes the pretext for a war against it, in which cause and perpetrator tend to converge in the shadowy figure of the elusive enemy" (102) is a tribute both to Weber's keen-sightedness and to the overdetermination of the "war on terror" as a notion and figure.

40. See, e.g., the speech of the Spartan king Archidamus in Thucydides' *Peloponnesian War*: a pragmatic soldier, Archidamus stresses that in war no calculation can predict what will happen because "it is impossible to calculate accurately [beforehand] events that are determined by chance [*tas prospiptousas tuchas ou logo diairetas*]" (1.84).

41. The German *Krieg*, meanwhile, according to the *Kluge Etymologisches Wörterbuch* (Berlin: de Gruyter, 1989), derives from words meaning variously "stubbornness," "persistence," "exertion," or "striving." Definitions of war

typically shuttle between invocations of form, order, and institution, on the one hand, and chaos and randomness, on the other. On the one hand, the confusion of war is often returned to the turbulent mystery of human nature: e.g., "Warfare is almost as old as man himself, and reaches into the most secret places of the human heart, places where self dissolves rational purpose, where pride reigns, where emotion is paramount, where instinct is king" (John Keegan, *A History of Warfare* [New York: Knopf, 1993], 3). On the other hand, stressing the difference between war and other sorts of violence, scholars emphasize the fundamental role of some degree of organization and goal-directedness, e.g.: "At the risk of grotesque simplification let me suggest that 'organized warfare' can best be defined with one word. That word is *formation*" (Arthur Ferrill, *The Origins of War from the Stone Age to Alexander the Great*, rev. ed. [Boulder, Colo.: Westview Press, 1997], 11).

42. Schmitt, *Nomos*, 320.

43. Daniel Pick, *The War Machine: The Rationalization of Slaughter in the Modern Age* (New Haven: Yale University Press, 1993), 106.

44. Ibid., 47. Pick's reference is to Clausewitz's notion of friction (a complementary trope to the more famous Clausewitzian "fog of war"): e.g., "The conduct of war resembles the workings of an intricate machine with tremendous friction, so that combinations which are easily planned on paper can be executed only with great effort" (Carl von Clausewitz, *Principles of War*, trans. Hans W. Gaske [Harrisburg, Pa.: The Stackpole Co., 1942], 50).

45. Jacqueline Rose, *Why War?—Psychoanalysis, Politics, and the Return to Melanie Klein* (Oxford: Blackwell, 1993), 16.

46. "The fog of war is quite literally noise, war's resistance to language, to objectification, to the code: both its problematic and its seductiveness, the limit of its intelligibility and the depth of its sublimity" (Paul Mann, *Masocriticism* [Albany: State University of New York Press, 1999], 119). For a shrewdly self-reflexive meditation on the figure of war in academic writing, see Mann's chapter "The Nine Grounds of Intellectual Warfare," 91–126.

47. Michel Foucault, *"Society Must Be Defended": Lectures at the Collège de France, 1975–76*, ed. Mauro Bertani and Allesandro Fontana (New York: Picador, 2003), 46.

48. Michel Foucault, "L'oeil de pouvoir," *Dits et écrits*, vol. 3 (Paris: Gallimard, 1994), 206; cited in Allesandro Fontana and Mauro Bertani, "Situating the Lectures," in Foucault, *"Society,"* 282.

49. Geoffrey Nunberg, "The -Ism Schism; How Much Wallop Can a Simple Word Pack?" *The New York Times*, Sunday, July 11, 2004, Week in Review, 7. I cannot vouch for the accuracy of Nunberg's claim about the relative frequency of use of these words in the media, but he is by profession a linguist and claims to have done some loosely empirical research: "In his speech of

[September 11, 2001], Mr. Bush said, 'We stand together to win the war against terrorism,' and over the following year the White House described the enemy as terrorism twice as often as terror. But in White House speeches over the past year, those proportions have been reversed. And the shift from 'terrorism' to 'terror' has been equally dramatic in major newspapers, according to the search of several databases."

50. Edmund Burke, *A Philosophical Enquiry into the Origin of Our Ideas of the Sublime and the Beautiful*, ed. James T. Boulton (Notre Dame, Ind.: University of Notre Dame Press, 1968), 40.

51. See Jacques Rancière, *Hatred of Democracy*, trans. Steve Corcoran (London: Verso, 2006). The argument can be made that even in France the Revolution has been celebrated more timidly in recent years than was the case in the first few decades after the Second World War, and that Robespierre and the Jacobins have been increasingly demonized: see Sophie Wahnich, *La liberté ou la mort: Essai sur la Terreur et le terrorisme* (Paris: La Fabrique, 2003).

52. Edmund Burke, *Four Letters on the Proposals for Peace with the Regicide Directory of France*, ed. E. J. Payne (Oxford: Oxford University Press, 1926), I, 87. Subsequent references to this text will be indicated by the short title *Regicide Peace*, plus letter and page number. It should be noted that Letter IV (referenced by the OED as containing the first use of the word "terrorist" in English, as noted above) was in fact the first of the four letters to be composed. It was written in December 1795 and acquired its misleading Roman numeral because it remained unpublished until 1812. Burke published Letters I and II together in 1796; Letter III appeared posthumously in 1797.

53. Schmitt does not say much about the French Revolution in his accounts of the breakdown of the *jus publicum Europaeum*, but he does consistently if glancingly note the "disruption" the Revolution caused in the "bracketing of land war between European sovereign states" (*Theory of the Partisan*, 9n10). On the rare occasion when he does mention the French Revolution in *The Nomos of the Earth*, his tone rises markedly: "The French Revolution spawned the words and concepts of Caesarism, civil war, dictatorship, and proletariat" (*Nomos*, 63).

54. Maximilien Robespierre, "Séance du 17 Pluviose An II (5 février 1794)," *Oeuvres de Maximilien Robespierre*, ed. Marc Bouloiseau and Albert Soboul (Paris: Presses Universitaires de France, 1912–67), 10:357. Here and elsewhere, unless otherwise noted, translations are mine.

55. Wahnich, *La liberté ou la mort*, 95. As Wahnich goes on to point out, even fervent republicans such as Victor Hugo distanced themselves from the Terror. During the nineteenth and twentieth centuries, over the course of a well-known history toward which I can only gesture here, the term "terror" came to be an all-purpose label to stigmatize groups who were challenging the

state's monopoly of violence. A few such groups have accepted and affirmed the terrorist label (e.g., the Russian anarchist movement of the 1880s; portions of the Zionist movement of the 1940s), but most, as noted at the beginning of this chapter, have sought recognition under other names.

56. Though for Robespierre, it should be recalled, "terror," as a synonym for "justice," is "an emanation of virtue." Terror expresses and serves virtue and is thus ultimately a means. Even the terrible Robespierre can only affirm terror as the instrument of a deeper moral principle. The Terror is thus also a "war on terror," not just because it targets real or imagined internal and external threats to the Revolution but because its violence can never be an end in itself (can never be, that is, what Benjamin calls "divine violence": the fractured telos of sovereignty). Later in this chapter I shall stress ways in which Robespierre and Burke mirror each other as emblematic political figures in the revolutionary landscape.

57. Arendt, *Origins*, 299.

58. Ibid., 297.

59. Agamben, *Homo Sacer*, 127. The concept of human rights, one of the most pressing issues of our era, has attracted subtle critical commentary: for a powerful collection of essays, see Ian Balfour and Eduardo Cadava, eds., *And Justice for All? The Claims of Human Rights*, special issue of *South Atlantic Quarterly* 103, no. 2/3 (Spring/Summer 2004).

60. Agamben, *Homo Sacer*, 171.

61. "Democracy" can, of course, be thought in many ways, and many rich texts have taken up the challenge of thinking a "radical democracy" resistant both to the pieties of bourgeois liberalism and to the temptations of a totalitarian mass politics. For a classic study, see Ernesto Laclau and Chantal Mouffe, *Hegemony and Socialist Strategy* (London: Verso, 1985), and the many subsequent books by these authors. Many texts could be mentioned; here let me only note, with respect to texts already cited in this chapter, that Rancière's *Hatred of Democracy* proposes a democracy that would be the "excess" of the political itself, while Derrida's *Rogues* offers a subtle exposition of the Derridean theme of "democracy to come"—a democracy fundamentally exposed to and hospitable toward the other.

62. Butler, *Precarious Life*, 62.

63. Brian Massumi, "Preface," in Brian Massumi, ed., *The Politics of Everyday Fear* (Minneapolis: University of Minnesota Press, 1993), vii.

64. In our contemporary bio-mapping of the body, fear's locus of manufacture is now understood to be in paths between nerve cells in the amygdala.

65. I echo here the well-known title of Elaine Scarry, *The Body in Pain: The Making and Unmaking of the World* (New York: Oxford University Press, 1985). As subsequent remarks will, I trust, make clear, my analysis of terror

as fear runs counter to Jean-Paul Sartre's important notes toward a phenomenology of fear, insofar as Sartre, as I read him, is describing emotions as intentional structures that presuppose a constituted world. "It is obvious indeed that
the man who is frightened is afraid *of* something," Sartre writes: see *Sketch for
a Theory of the Emotions*, trans. Philip Mairet (London: Methuen, 1962), 56–57.
Fear's relation to its object is one of flight; fainting is an intentional act because
it constitutes a denial of the threat's existence for consciousness; and Sartre in
fact goes so far as to make literal running away phenomenologically derivative
of fainting: "Flight is fainting away in action; it is magical behavior which
negates the dangerous object with one's whole body" (67). These are shrewd
observations, but they presuppose consciousness and its world, whereas I think
we touch upon a deeper moment of exposure to "that which is" in the extreme
state of fear we call terror. Such terror is better described by Heidegger's
concept of mood or attunement, invoked below.

66. Sigmund Freud, *Group Psychology and the Analysis of the Ego*, in *The
Standard Edition of the Complete Psychological Works of Sigmund Freud*, trans.
James Strachey (London: The Hogarth Press, 1955), 18:95–96. In recent years,
good critical work has been done on the irreducibility of affect to individual
subjectivity: an idea that, while as old as that of passion itself, may be returned
under the terms of a more restricted genealogy to Heidegger's seminal writing
on mood. On the irreducibility of affect to individual identity, see, in the field
of literary criticism, Adela Pinch, *Strange Fits of Passion: Epistemologies of Emotion, Hume to Austen* (Stanford: Stanford University Press, 1996), and Rei Terada, *Feeling in Theory: Emotion after the "Death of the Subject"* (Cambridge:
Harvard University Press, 2001).

67. Martin Heidegger, *Grundbegriffe der Metaphysik: Welt—Endlichkeit—
Einsamkeit*, Gesamtausgabe (Frankfurt am Main: Vittorio Klostermann, 1983),
vol. 29/30; *The Fundamental Concepts of Metaphysics: World, Finitude, Solitude*,
trans. William McNeill and Nicholas Walker (Bloomington: Indiana University Press, 1995), 66. The seminar is that of the winter semester, 1929–30.

68. I shall have to defer an analysis of Heidegger's *The Fundamental Concepts of Metaphysics* to another occasion, but it may be remarked here that in
this important text, which substitutes a focus on boredom for *Being and Time*'s
focus on anxiety, Heidegger repeatedly calls for terror as the antidote required
by a degenerate society—a disturbing emphasis, in 1929–30: "The mystery
[*Geheimnis*] is lacking in our Dasein, and thereby the inner terror [*innere
Schrecken*] that every mystery carries with it and that gives Dasein its greatness
remains absent. The absence of oppressiveness is what fundamentally op-
presses and leaves us profoundly empty, i.e., the *fundamental emptiness that
bores us*" (244/164, italics in original); "We must first call for someone capable
of instilling terror [*Schrecken*] into our Dasein again. For how do things stand

with our Dasein, when an event like the Great War can to all extents and purposes pass us by without leaving a trace?" (255–56/172). Philosophy, for Heidegger, is an encounter with terror: "This is merely idle talk that talks in a direction leading away from philosophy. We must rather uphold and hold out in this terror [Schrecken]. For in it there becomes manifest something essential about all philosophical comprehension, namely that in the philosophical concept, man and indeed man as a whole, is in the grip of an attack—driven out of everydayness and driven back into the ground of things. Yet the attacker is not man, the dubious subject of the everyday and of the bliss of knowledge. Rather, *in philosophizing the Da-sein in man launches the attack upon man*" (31/21, italics in original). A close reading of the seminar would, I believe, show that, although Heidegger of course understands attunement as prior to subjectivity, a creeping voluntarism in his text weakens his analysis in ways that both map onto the temptation that National Socialism was to pose for his thought and vitiate the analysis of attunement precisely to the extent that the notion of "terror" in sentences like those cited above remains unexamined. Extreme boredom, in this text, reveals being (and is therefore the privilege of the human: the animal, poor in world [weltarm] cannot truly be bored). Does terror? Heidegger suggests that extreme boredom *is* terror; but perhaps it would become necessary to discover in terror an excess beyond the possibility of disclosure—to understand terror as both *Stimmung*'s condition of possibility and, in a certain sense, its ruin.

69. Søren Kierkegaard, *The Concept of Irony, with Continual Reference to Socrates*, ed. and trans. Howard V. Hong and Edna H. Hong (Princeton: Princeton University Press, 1989). In Heidegger's *Fundamental Concepts of Metaphysics*, one must qualify, the animal is *not* capable of experiencing terror, insofar as terror is aligned with the extreme boredom that reveals being and with the wonder that is the life of true philosophy: "And only because he is thus mistaken and transposed can [man] be *seized by terror*. And only where there is the perilousness of being seized by terror do we find the bliss of astonishment—being torn away in that wakeful manner that is the breath of all philosophizing, and which the greats among the philosophers called *enthousiasmos*" (366); "Und nur weil so versehen und versetzt, kann er sich *entsetzen*. Und nur, wo die Gefährlichkeit des Entsetzens, da die Seligkeit des Staunens—jene wache Hingerissenheit, die der Odem alles Philosophierens ist, und was die Grössten der Philosophen den *enthousiasmos* nannten" (531). Heidegger's play on words is hard to translate: *entsetzen* means "to frighten," while the reflexive *sich entsetzen* means "to get a fright": one is human because one can *give oneself terror*, which is also to say, hold oneself open to terror.

70. For brilliant discussions of trauma as "the inability fully to witness the event as it occurs, or the ability to witness the event fully only at the cost of

witnessing oneself," see the work of Cathy Caruth; I quote here from her introduction to *Trauma: Explorations in Memory*, ed. Cathy Caruth (Baltimore: Johns Hopkins University Press, 1995), 7; see also her *Unclaimed Experience: Trauma, Narrative, and History* (Baltimore: Johns Hopkins University Press, 1996).

71. Jacques Derrida, *The Politics of Friendship*, trans. George Collins (London: Verso, 1997), 173–74.

72. Derrida, "Autoimmunity," 97. As noted in the previous chapter, this observation is a common one in intelligent writing about the September 11 attacks. Slavoj Žižek writes, for instance, that "the true long-term threat is further acts of mass terror in comparison with which the memory of the WTC collapse will pale—acts that are less spectacular, but much more horrifying. . . . We are entering a new era of paranoiac warfare in which the greatest task will be to identify the enemy and his weapons" (*Welcome to the Desert of the Real! Five Essays on September 11 and Related Dates* [London: Verso, 2002], 36–37).

73. Primo Levi, *Survival in Auschwitz*, trans. Stuart Woolf (1959; New York: Collier Books, 1986), 62.

74. Arendt, *Origins*, 300.

75. W. G. Sebald, *On the Natural History of Destruction*, trans. Anthea Bell (New York: Random House, 2003), 53.

76. Jean Paulhan, *Les fleurs de Tarbes, ou, La terreur dans les letters* (Paris: Gallimard, 1941), 53.

77. Maurice Blanchot, "Comment la littérature est-elle possible?" in *Faux Pas* (Paris: Gallimard, 1943), 97.

78. Perhaps a thumbnail sketch of Kojève's anthropomorphic reading of Hegel's master-slave dialectic is in order. In this narrative, the two subjects who are to become master and slave enter into a deadly fight for recognition; the subject who risks his life utterly becomes the master, and the subject who doesn't becomes the slave. The master thus, as master, personifies terror—more specifically, the fear of death—for the slave. He forces the slave to work; working causes the slave to attain genuine, technical, mediate mastery of the world, as opposed to the master's immediate mastery; thus, ultimately, the slave becomes the master's master, the master of the world. Mapping this mythico-theoretical narrative onto history, Kojève claims that the modern state emerges in and as the Terror of the French Revolution. See Alexandre Kojève, *Introduction to the Reading of Hegel*, trans. James H. Nichols, Jr. (Ithaca: Cornell University Press, 1969), 3–30, 69, passim.

79. Maurice Blanchot, "Literature and the Right to Death," trans. Lydia Davis, in *The Work of Fire*, trans. Charlotte Mandell (Stanford: Stanford University Press, 1995), 313.

80. Though Blanchot is certainly not offering a sociological account here, his and Paulhan's rendering of Jacobin ideology has historical purchase. On the importance of a certain ideal of communicational and representational transparency in Jacobin rhetoric, see Lynn Hunt's classic study *Politics, Culture, and Class in the French Revolution* (Berkeley: University of California Press, 1984), esp. 19–51. The effort to break absolutely with the past, Hunt suggests, invested language with "sacred authority" (26); meanwhile, the effort to make democracy as immediate as possible in Jacobin circles was of a piece with the presumptive transparency of charged words (patriot, virtue, etc.) and a Rousseauist emphasis on sentiment and conscience. As Hunt emphasizes, the Jacobin stress on transparency was equally an obsession with conspiracy. The Terror, she goes so far as to suggest, "followed logically from the presuppositions of revolutionary language" (46)—from the double fealty to, on the one hand, rhetoric and the power of the spoken word, and, on the other hand, the abolition of all rhetoric and mediation in the name of transparency.

81. William Wordsworth, *The Prelude: 1799, 1805, 1850*, ed. Jonathan Wordsworth, M. H. Abrams, and Stephen Gill (New York: W. W. Norton, 1979), 1850 version, 7:527–30, my italics. Wordsworth probably drafted these lines between 1820 and 1828. For discussion, see James K. Chandler, *Wordsworth's Second Nature: A Study of the Poetry and Politics* (Chicago: University of Chicago Press, 1984), esp. 15–16.

82. Edmund Burke, "Thoughts on French Affairs" (1791), in *Further Reflections on the Revolution in France*, ed. Daniel E. Ritchie (Indianapolis: Liberty Fund, 1993), 208; see also 213–15. Later in this chapter a number of texts by Burke will be cited from Ritchie's collection: "Letter to Philip Francis" (1790); "An Appeal from the New to the Old Whigs" (1791); "A Letter to a Member of the National Assembly" (1791); "Letter to William Elliot" (1795); "A Letter to a Noble Lord" (1796). My references to Burke's *Reflections on the Revolution in France* (1790) are to the edition edited by Conor Cruise O'Brien (New York: Penguin, 1986).

83. David Simpson, *Romanticism, Nationalism, and the Revolt Against Theory* (Chicago: University of Chicago Press, 1993), 173. See also Neil Hertz, *The End of the Line: Essays on Psychoanalysis and the Sublime* (New York: Columbia University Press, 1985), for a trenchant analysis of the "resistance to theory" from the romantic era to the present. Simpson, for his part, usefully associates the American academy's resistance to Paul de Man with a nationalist resistance to "radical cosmopolitanism" (180), which resonates with the Burkean resistance to the Jacobin threat. He also sees theory as associated with a dangerous levelling tendency in the form of a rationalist assault on custom and habit (see Simpson, *Romanticism*, 38–39). I provide an extensive analysis of de Man's

role as the embodiment of "theory" in *The Politics of Aesthetics*, esp. 1–42 and 95–124.

84. Paul de Man, *Allegories of Reading: Figural Language in Rousseau, Nietzsche, Rilke, and Proust* (New Haven: Yale University Press, 1979), 151. See my *Politics of Aesthetics* for a more extensive account of these issues; see also Terada's *Feeling in Theory* for a fine reading of this chapter and of de Man's work generally that emphasizes the degree to which de Man's work theorizes and thematizes emotion.

85. As Terada nicely puts it, "If we have emotions because we can't know what to believe (what texts and people are up to) as de Man suggests, then we have emotions even though we can't know which emotions we ought to have. If we truly *knew* which emotions we should have, we would no longer feel like having any" (*Feeling in Theory*, 89). The (self-defacing) name of that non-knowing in de Man, I think, is "fear" or "terror." De Man's work not infrequently returns to the theme of terror's uncertain ontology, which is also that of reading. In "Hypogram and Inscription," de Man characterizes Saussure's uncertain perception of anagrammatic pattern in Latin poetry as "a terror glimpsed": see *The Resistance to Theory* (Minneapolis: University of Minnesota Press, 1986), 37. Improvising in "Kant and Schiller," de Man develops an extended riff on the sort of "terror" Kant might have felt when approaching the materiality of the letter—but again the point is that this terror is not something we can claim to know anything about: "I don't think that Kant, when he wrote about the heavens and the sea there, that he was shuddering in mind. Any literalism there would not be called for. It is terrifying in a way we don't know " (*Aesthetic Ideology* [Minneapolis: University of Minnesota Press, 1996], 134). My claim here is that it is critically useful to think of terror as essentially linked to uncertainty. Hannah Arendt's version of the Rousseauist parable in *Origins of Totalitarianism* offers a cautionary instance: "The Boers," she claims—seeking an etiology for racism in South Africa—"were never able to forget their first horrible fright before a species of men whom human pride and the sense of human dignity could not allow them to accept as fellow men" (192; cf. 195, 197). This is a reductive moment in Arendt's brilliant book; it would be more critically useful, I think, to thematize racism (in this fictional scenario) as a further freezing whereby the "giant" of Rousseau is resurrected as the literal, and abjected, body of the other.

86. John Searle, "The Word Turned Upside Down," *New York Review of Books*, October 27, 1983, 77.

87. Such is the thesis of, among others, Conor Cruise O'Brien, who in his intelligent introduction to the Penguin edition of the *Reflections* teases out links between Burke's conservatism and the complexities of Anglo-Irish identity: "his power to penetrate the processes of the revolution derives from a

suppressed sympathy with revolution, combined with an intuitive grasp of the subversive possibilities of *counter*-revolutionary propaganda, as affecting the established order in the land of his birth" (81). As so often, one can go to Novalis for a rich epigram: "Many antirevolutionary books have been written in favor of the Revolution. Burke, however, wrote a revolutionary book against the Revolution" (Friedrich von Hardenberg [Novalis], *Blütenstaub*, no. 115, in *Novalis Werke*, ed. Gerhard Schulz [Munich: C. H. Beck, 1981], 349).

88. Burke, *Reflections*, 195.

89. Ibid.

90. Burke frequently claims that his principles are grounded in religion, and more specifically Christianity: "religion is the basis of civil society"; "man is by his constitution a religious animal" (*Reflections*, 186, 187). The latter formulation shades into the Burkean anthropological-pragmatic claim about religion: whether or not religion is true, it is natural and good that we have it. Religion, like all else, is both affirmed and rendered fictional.

91. Burke, "An Appeal from the New to the Old Whigs," 163–64.

92. Ibid., 169. Thus, because Burke's conservatism is all about mediation, in opposition to the immediacy of revolution and terror, his aesthetic ideology can take Coleridgean form as a celebration of the symbol: see, e.g., Ritchie's neo-Burkean claim that Burke "symboliz[es] the Constitution as Coleridge defines 'symbol'"—as the "transluscence of the Eternal through and in the Temporal." Thus, Ritchie says, "the individual elements of the nation (King, Lords, Commons) participate in the unity of the Constitution without losing their identity" (Burke, *Further Reflections*, xx), producing "a union of the spirit and the flesh" (xxi). For a more rigorous discussion of the similarities between Coleridge's organicist aesthetic of the symbol and Burke's political writing, see Tom Furniss, *Edmund Burke's Aesthetic Ideology: Language, Gender, and Political Economy in Revolution* (Cambridge: Cambridge University Press, 1993), 228 and passim.

93. Burke, *Reflections*, 120.

94. Ibid., 110–11.

95. Ibid., 116. One encounters the charged figure of the potentially self-erasing line throughout Burke's writings on the Revolution: e.g., "duties, at their extreme bounds, are drawn very fine, so as to become almost evanescent" ("An Appeal from the New to the Old Whigs," 162). Sometimes anti-Semitism marks the threat of a dissolving border; see, e.g., "A Letter to a Member of the National Assembly," in which the Jew is linked to pollution across borders, and to forgery, housebreaking, and stolen goods (39); Mahomet is also mentioned as a prototype of the revolutionary (40–41).

96. See Martin Heidegger, "Die Frage nach der Technik," in *Vorträge und Aufsätze* (Tübingen: Günther Neske, 1954), 13–44: "Steuerung und Sicherung

werden sogar die Hauptzüge des herausfordernden Entbergens" (24). For the English, see "The Question Concerning Technology" in *The Question Concerning Technology and Other Essays*, trans. William Lovitt (New York: Harper Torchbooks, 1977), 3–35: "Regulating and securing even become the chief characteristics of the challenging revealing" (16).

97. Kant, *Toward Perpetual Peace*, 107.

98. Immanuel Kant, "The End of All Things," in *Perpetual Peace and Other Essays*, 98. We fall into mysticism if we imagine that we can gain properly cognitive knowledge of eternity: in thus stepping beyond its limits, reason ceases to understand itself. Kant threatens us with dire consequences if we indulge in such excesses: we might become "Chinese philosophers" or apocalyptic enthusiasts (99–100). Figural representations of what happens "after" the Last Day are "sensuous representations" of something that cannot be conceived theoretically and cannot even be expressed in language without strain: timelessness blurs into petrification, and thoughtful speech crumbles into the stutter of Hallelujah or lamentation (99).

99. Peter Fenves, *Late Kant: Toward Another Law of the Earth* (New York: Routledge, 2003), 92.

100. Much of Kant's text could be said to be acting out the dark pun sleeping in the German word *Friedensschluß* ("peace treaty," but also, if broken up into its components, "end of peace"). Should nations, for instance, commit unforgivable war crimes, a "war of extermination . . . would permit perpetual peace to occur only in the vast graveyard of humanity as a whole" (*Toward Perpetual Peace*, 110); should the prudent advocates of *Realpolitik* be allowed a hearing, their "damaging theory may bring about the evil that it prophesizes, for in it man is thrown into the same class as other living machines, which need only to become conscious that they are not free in order to become in their own eyes the most wretched of all the earth's creatures" (133). The terrible imperative of the moral law itself can at times seem in danger of leading us toward the universal graveyard that flickers repeatedly into view: *Fiat iustia, pereat mundus*: let justice reign, even if all the rogues in the world should perish, as Kant translates the proverb (133). And at times Kant tells us that the world deserves the wars it wages: "When one person violates the rights of another who is just as lawlessly disposed toward him, then whatever happens to them as they destroy themselves is entirely right; enough of their race will always survive so that this game will not cease, even into the remotest age, and they can serve as a warning to later generations" (134). Such apocalyptic imaginings of the end of all things cannot be expunged from the moral imperative to perpetual peace, because perpetual peace cannot properly be thought, figured, or imagined. Yet it is important to keep in mind that the graveyard, though an ineluctable figure of the aporia of perpetual peace—an inevitable

image on the signboard bearing the inscription *Zum ewigen Frieden*—is nonetheless not this inscription's proper or literal meaning. Peace does not have a proper meaning. I am arguing here that in its radical figurativeness, peace opens the fragile possibility of another peacetime, opening enlightenment to a millenarianism without millenarianism, by way of an imperative that urges pragmatic action, not despite but because of the volatile figurativeness of peace.

101. In Kantian terms, the thought of eternity extends knowledge in a moral context, and moral imperatives call out for practical action. It is therefore tempting to call peace a regulative idea of practical reason—a corollary to the regulative ideas of freedom, God, and immortality. But though the regulative ideas of freedom, God, and immortality may be said to be accomplishments of practical reason, these ideas do not refer to political states of existence to be realized empirically (however impossibly) through a speech act. Peace remains bound up not just with political action but with the performative force of language—and thus with the perpetual possibility of ruinous failure. We might say (adapting the formulation offered by David L. Clark that I am about to quote) that Kant proceeds *as if* peace could be a regulative idea.

102. David L. Clark, *Bodies and Pleasures in Late Kant* (Stanford: Stanford University Press, forthcoming). Clark's powerful reading of *Toward Perpetual Peace*, which forms part of his wider survey of Kant's late writing, notes the paradox of the peace declaration—that one must be at peace in order to make the declaration that produces peace (i.e., one must be *zum*, in, *ewigen Frieden*, in order to move *zum*, toward it; furthermore, as we have noted, none of these movements are properly thinkable)—and proposes that we understand peace as a promise, a trusting in trust, a hospitable opening: that we read Kant's text as a testimonial to the testimonial act called peace. See his concluding chapter, "Imagining Peace: Kant's Wartime and the Tremulous Body of Philosophy."

103. Fenves, *Late Kant*, 111.

INDEX